EVERYTHING YOU NEED TO KNOW TO BE A SUCCESSFUL WHOLE LANGUAGE TEACHER

Plans, Strategies, Techniques, & More

by Judith Cochran

Incentive Publications, Inc.
Nashville, Tennessee

Illustrated by Gayle Seaberg Harvey
Cover by Geoffrey Brittingham
Edited by Leslie Britt

Library of Congress Catalog Card Number: 93-077472
ISBN 0-86530-236-7

Table of Contents

OVERVIEW

Everything You Need to Know to Be a Successful Whole Language Teacher is an easy-to-use, hands-on manual designed to familiarize teachers with the fundamental principles of whole language. By examining the basic concepts of whole language and by showing how these concepts can be successfully implemented in every K-6 classroom, *Everything You Need to Know* demystifies this important field of instruction.

The bulk of this work is devoted to a study of the four principal curricular skills of listening, speaking, reading and comprehension, and writing. A Scope and Sequence Chart of Whole Language Skills breaks down these areas into their component parts. Each skill is then examined in-depth. In addition to highlighting recent research outlined in the landmark study *Becoming a Nation of Readers,* step-by-step instructions and specific activities geared to each skill area are provided. All activities and instructional strategies are categorized according to level of difficulty: emergent learners (approximately grades K-1), developing learners (approximately grades 2-3), and fluent learners (approximately grades 4-6). These sample activities can help teachers build the foundation of their own whole language programs.

This resource also addresses a variety of curricular-related issues, such as setting up the classroom for optimal learning, employing a broad range of grouping techniques and strategies, pre-, during, and post-lesson activities to enhance students' learning, implementing basals and workbooks, and the effective introduction of parents to the whole language classroom. A chapter on evaluating whole language programs offers teachers a wide range of assessment techniques. In addition, book lists are provided for emergent, developing, and fluent learners.

The basic tenets of a whole language program are similar to those of any good child-centered classroom. With *Everything You Need to Know to Be a Successful Whole Language Teacher,* interested teachers will have not only the materials but the know-how to start their own successful programs!

Chapter One

WHAT IS WHOLE LANGUAGE?

There is nothing mysterious about whole language. It is simply a systematic approach to instruction using real-life learning situations which enable children to conceive of reading and writing as life skills rather than as isolated bits of information. Good teachers have understood and implemented whole language instruction for some time. It is only during the past few years, however, that national education researchers have caught up with them. Their research is summed up in the ground-breaking report *Becoming a Nation of Readers* commissioned by the United States Department of Education. The report presents, for the first time, a synthesis of the integral units of a good whole language program—literature-based reading, numerous opportunities for students to listen, speak, read and write, and instruction based on themes.

Most teachers already use many aspects of whole language instruction in their classrooms. The purpose of this book is to identify and clarify the basic concepts and methods of whole language instruction, promote an increase in the classroom use of these methods, and offer some new ideas as well. All of the activities presented in this book are outlined on the chart entitled "Scope and Sequence of Whole Language Skills" (pages 16-17).

A good whole language program should consist of a few basic elements which can be implemented in the classroom in a variety of ways. Every kindergarten through sixth grade whole language classroom should have:

- **Read Aloud Time:** Time should be set aside during the day for the teacher to read works of literature aloud to students.

- **Silent Reading:** A sustained period of time should be set aside every day for children to choose books and read them quietly.

- **Daily Writing Experiences:** Children should have ample opportunities to write about themselves, their thoughts, and their reading assignments.

- **Speaking Opportunities:** Provide speaking opportunities and oral presentations in whole group, small group, and one-on-one situations.

- **Thematic Approach To Teaching:** Classroom instruction and student activities should be based on units of study and not individual subject areas.

Research reveals that children learn best from experiencing whole processes. A child's mind is not constructed from building blocks, one upon the other. A child cannot receive knowledge a piece at a time and make any sense out of it. It is only when ideas and activities are dealt with as whole entities that children can truly learn and apply their knowledge in real, meaningful ways. Children learn to read by reading themselves, and they learn to write by writing. This holistic approach to learning is the cornerstone of a good whole language program.

Whole language instruction is based on the natural process by which children learn and encompasses all the ways children naturally receive and express information. The whole language program then structures teaching methods according to these natural processes using literature as the basis for complete units of instruction.

What is the natural learning process? One of the first steps children take is learning how to speak. They do this naturally by hearing language spoken, coming to understand words, and finally speaking themselves.

CHILD HEARS LANGUAGE   CHILD RECEIVES AND
                            UNDERSTANDS LANGUAGE

CHILD SPEAKS LANGUAGE

Language that is received and understood is referred to as *receptive* language; spoken language is referred to as *expressive* language. Elementary and middle school students usually understand more language then they can express. In other words, their receptive language is greater than their expressive language. Teachers should read literature aloud to their students and present whole units of instruction in order for children to receive and comprehend entire concepts.

By the time most children have learned to speak and have a basic command of language, they enter school. In a whole language program, the teacher continues to nurture this natural learning process by structuring the information the students receive, helping them process that information, and encouraging them to express themselves through speaking and writing.

Throughout grades K-6, teachers will encourage and develop this natural learning process differently, depending on their students' ability levels. Of course, a child in kindergarten or first grade has abilities which are quite different from those of a child in the fifth or sixth grade. For this reason, the activities in this book are divided into three sections according to different stages of development.

- **Emergent Learners** (approximately grades K-1)
  These are children who do not read or write well, but are becoming aware of the basics involved in accomplishing these processes.

- **Developing Learners** (approximately grades 2-3)
  These students have mastered basic reading and writing skills and can understand information they read. The stories they read and write have become more detailed and complex.

- **Fluent Learners** (approximately grades 4-6)
  Fluent learners are confident readers and writers. They are able to use many strategies to read and write a variety of stories intended for different audiences.

EMERGENT LEARNERS (Approximately Grades K-1)

The four basic components of whole language instruction are listening, speaking, reading, and writing. People receive information by reading and listening and express information by writing and speaking. Because emergent learners are not yet able to read and write very well, they must depend upon on their listening and speaking skills in order to acquire knowledge. It is only through the modalities of listening and speaking that the whole language teacher can structure activities to teach emergent learners how to read and, later, to write.

RECEIVE
listening
reading

EXPRESS
speaking
writing

Emergent learners are beginning to understand the connection between the words they hear and speak and the words written in a book. The whole language teacher must provide many experiences which help their students understand that connection and understand the meanings of the words. A chart of the emergent child's natural learning process with teacher input might look like this:

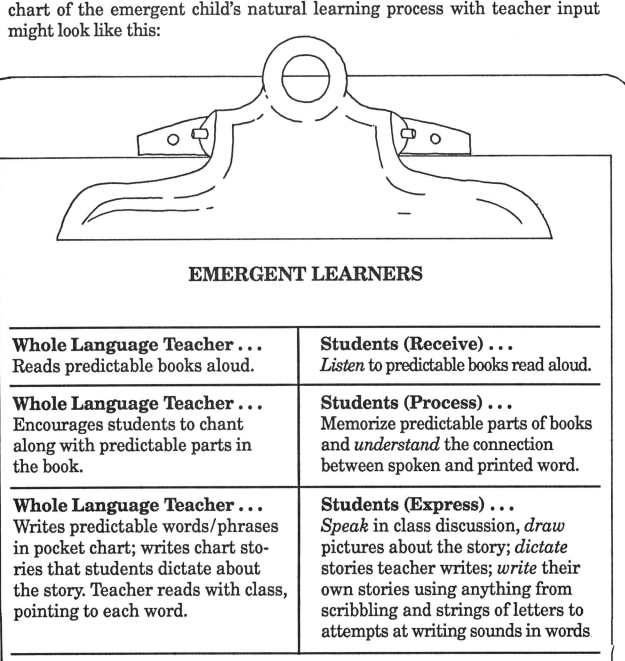

EMERGENT LEARNERS

Whole Language Teacher...	**Students (Receive)...**
Reads predictable books aloud.	*Listen* to predictable books read aloud.
Whole Language Teacher... Encourages students to chant along with predictable parts in the book.	**Students (Process)...** Memorize predictable parts of books and *understand* the connection between spoken and printed word.
Whole Language Teacher... Writes predictable words/phrases in pocket chart; writes chart stories that students dictate about the story. Teacher reads with class, pointing to each word.	**Students (Express)...** *Speak* in class discussion, *draw* pictures about the story; *dictate* stories teacher writes; *write* their own stories using anything from scribbling and strings of letters to attempts at writing sounds in words.

This chart represents only a portion of the methods a whole language teacher might use to instruct emergent learners. More detailed activities are provided in the chapters on listening (pages 46-49), reading (pages 50-83), and writing (pages 84-107). This example does illustrate, however, a few of the many listening, speaking, and beginning reading and writing activities available for children just learning how to read.

Developing learners have already mastered the basics of reading and writing. Their instruction should be focused on reading comprehension. A chart of the developing learner's natural learning process with teacher input might look like this:

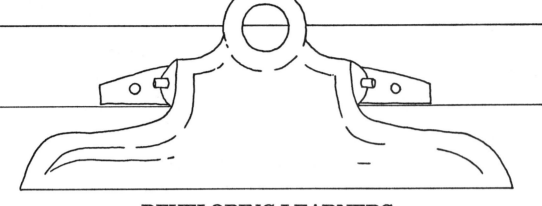

DEVELOPING LEARNERS

Whole Language Teacher . . . Reads aloud often, asking students to listen for specifics in stories. Gives students the purpose for reading a story.	Students (Receive) . . . *Listen* to stories and read stories.
Whole Language Teacher . . . Encourages students to predict events in story, discuss character, setting, cause/effect, etc.	Students (Process) . . . *Understand* story elements, character, setting, plot, etc.
Whole Language Teacher . . . Discusses character, setting, plot specifics; makes story frames (character, setting, plot); asks students to retell story or sequence events.	Students (Express) . . . *Speak* about and *act out* characters in story; *write* reaction to story aspects, noting similarities, differences between characters, etc.

This is only a sample of the developing learner's experiences. More detailed activities are discussed in the chapters on listening (pages 46-49), reading (pages 50-83), and writing (pages 84-107). It is essential to keep in mind that meaning is being constructed for the students by the teacher who adds to and reinforces each part of the natural learning process.

Fluent learners are confident readers and writers who can easily construct meaning from their reading assignments. Most of their time should be spent reading a variety of material, developing strategies for comprehending their reading, and writing responses to it. A chart of the fluent learner's natural learning process with teacher input might look like this:

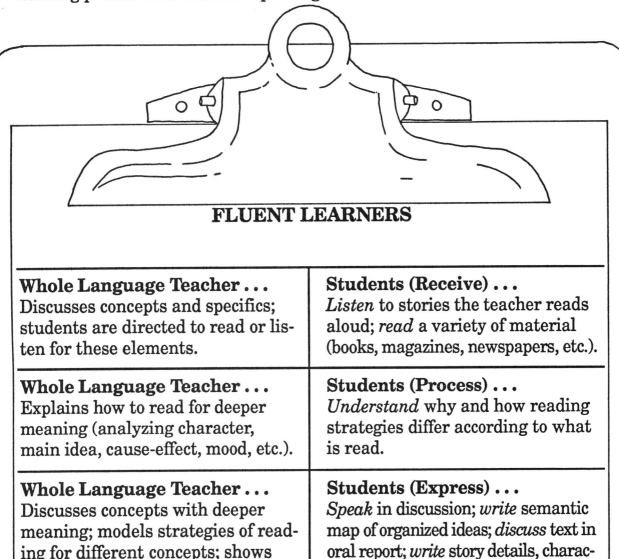

FLUENT LEARNERS

Whole Language Teacher . . . Discusses concepts and specifics; students are directed to read or listen for these elements.	**Students (Receive) . . .** *Listen* to stories the teacher reads aloud; *read* a variety of material (books, magazines, newspapers, etc.).
Whole Language Teacher . . . Explains how to read for deeper meaning (analyzing character, main idea, cause-effect, mood, etc.).	**Students (Process) . . .** *Understand* why and how reading strategies differ according to what is read.
Whole Language Teacher . . . Discusses concepts with deeper meaning; models strategies of reading for different concepts; shows how to organize ideas for reports.	**Students (Express) . . .** *Speak* in discussion; *write* semantic map of organized ideas; *discuss* text in oral report; *write* story details, character analysis, cause-effect, mood, etc.

Remember that it is important to discuss step-by-step with fluent learners how to find such story elements as the main idea, character traits, author's intent, etc. More detailed activities are discussed in the chapters on listening (pages 46-49), reading (pages 50-83), and writing (pages 84-107).

Emergent, developing, and fluent learners need a great deal of experience with all four elements of whole language—listening, speaking, reading, and writing. As the three previous learning charts demonstrate, none of these aspects can be separated from the others. All four are inextricably linked. That the whole language program takes this into account is what makes it fundamentally different from a traditional approach to learning.

Listening   Speaking   Reading   Writing

In traditional school programs, students spend too much of the school day in a receptive mode, not actively involved in processing information or expressing their knowledge. Traditional reading programs are more concerned with product than with process. For example, a teacher might emphasize how many right or wrong answers a child produced on a workbook assignment rather than spending the time to teach the child how to glean the main idea of a selection. In effect, traditional programs test pupils on a main idea without teaching them how to arrive at it. In recent years, basal reading programs have sought to address this issue and have put more emphasis on thinking processes and written expression. Many of them provide a solid foundation for a good whole language program.

Whole language, on the other hand, emphasizes process over product. It stresses the importance of thinking by giving students concrete activities requiring concrete solutions. The way in which children process their thoughts is observed in their writing and speaking. By evaluating these processes, teachers are able to see in which areas their students are functioning well and poorly and adjust their methods of instruction accordingly.

Listening, speaking, reading, and writing are interrelated processes; therefore, for true learning to take place, a teacher must introduce students to all of these concepts at the same time. These two modality webs illustrate this idea. The web on the left reveals the lack of reinforcement evident in the traditional vocabulary/reader/workbook approach to reading instruction. The web on the right demonstrates the cross-pollination of modalities found in a whole language program.

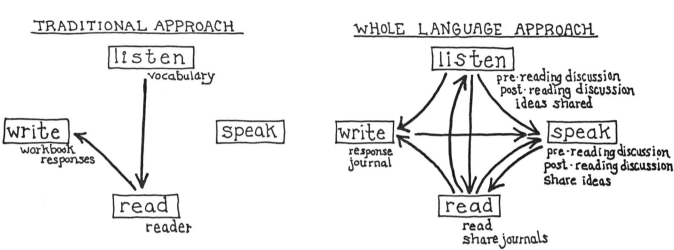

MODALITY WEBS

TRADITIONAL APPROACH

listen
vocabulary

write
workbook
responses

speak

read
reader

WHOLE LANGUAGE APPROACH

listen
pre-reading discussion
post-reading discussion
ideas shared

write
response
journal

speak
pre-reading discussion
post-reading discussion
share ideas

read
read
share journals

In a typical whole language lesson, the learning process is enhanced by all the modalities being brought into play. Between the students' discussion and their reading and writing, the whole language teacher can clearly see just how well a student is functioning or whether that student needs additional instruction on a particular concept. In contrast, the traditional teacher has little more to go by than the limited answers produced on a workbook page.

SCOPE AND SEQUENCE OF WHOLE LANGUAGE SKILLS, K-6

This scope and sequence chart of whole language skills has been formulated to assist teachers in covering the basic skills and concepts important in all K-6 whole language programs. It is not intended to be used as a checklist, but rather as a guide. Specific strategies for teaching these concepts in a whole language program are outlined in the chapters on listening (pages 46-49), reading (pages 50-83), and writing (pages 84-107).

SCOPE AND SEQUENCE CHART OF WHOLE LANGUAGE SKILLS, K-6

Grades	Emerging		Developing		Fluent		
	K	1	2	3	4	5	6

LISTENING

Students Listen as Teacher Reads Aloud Daily	x	x	x	x	x	x	x
Students Have Daily Opportunities to Listen	x	x	x	x	x	x	x

SPEAKING

Students Have Daily Opportunities to Speak	x	x	x	x	x	x	x

READING

	K	1	2	3	4	5	6
Teacher Reads Aloud Daily	x	x	x	x	x	x	x
Students Read Silently Every Day	x	x	x	x	x	x	x
Students Read in Other Situations Daily	x	x	x	x	x	x	x
Word Identification							
• phonics (vowels/consonants)	x	x	x				
• contractions, compound words		x	x	x			
• sight words		x	x	x			
Vocabulary							
• recognize word meanings	x	x	x	x	x	x	x
• roots, prefixes, suffixes	x	x	x	x	x	x	x
• synonyms/antonyms	x	x	x	x	x	x	x
• unfamiliar words in context	x	x	x	x	x	x	x
Comprehension							
Literal							
• details	x	x	x	x	x	x	x
• pronoun reference	x	x	x	x	x	x	x
• sequence	x	x	x	x	x	x	x
Inferential							
• relate story to personal experiences	x	x	x	x	x	x	x
• main idea	x	x	x	x	x	x	x
• cause/effect	x	x	x	x	x	x	x

READING (Continued)

	Emerging		Developing		Fluent		
Grades	K	1	2	3	4	5	6
• draw conclusions	x	x	x	x	x	x	x
• predict outcomes	x	x	x	x	x	x	x
• compare/contrast	x	x	x	x	x	x	x
Critical Thinking							
• analyze character, setting	x	x	x	x	x	x	x
• real/make-believe		x	x	x			
• summarize plot			x	x	x	x	x
• fact/opinion					x	x	x
• mood						x	x
• author's tone/intent						x	x
Study Skills							
• maps/charts/graphs	x	x	x	x	x	x	x
• book parts (table of contents/title page/index)	x	x	x	x	x	x	x
• alphabetization			x	x			
• dictionary			x	x	x	x	x
• reference (newspaper/telephone book/ encyclopedia/atlas)			x	x	x	x	x
• card catalog				x	x	x	x

WRITING

	Emerging		Developing		Fluent		
	K	1	2	3	4	5	6
Students Write Every Day							
journal/informal/formal writing experiences	x	x	x	x	x	x	x
Spelling							
• invented	x	x	x	x			
• formal		x	x	x	x	x	x
Sentences/Paragraphs							
• teacher writes dictated sentences	x	x	x				
• students complete sentence/story frames	x	x	x				
• write original sentences/paragraphs		x	x	x	x	x	x
• use vivid words (adjectives/adverbs/verbs)		x	x	x	x	x	x
• capitalization/punctuation/grammar		x	x	x	x	x	x
• letter form (personal/business)		x	x	x	x	x	x
• poetry		x	x	x	x	x	x
• organize information for paragraphs/reports			x	x	x	x	x

A number of misconceptions have made teachers wary of whole language instruction. They include the beliefs that:

• You must throw out all of your materials and start over.
• Small groups are a sin.
• No basal texts or workbooks are allowed.
• Kids are out of control.
• No basic skills are taught.
• It involves too much work for teachers.

Whole language does not involve any of this! These misconceptions have been fueled by a few zealots who believe whole language can be taught only one way. In truth, the implementation of a whole language program has as many faces as there are teachers using it. To further clear up these misunderstandings, let's discuss them one at a time:

You Must Throw Out All Of Your Materials And Start Over. No, keep them! Chances are you already have many aspects of a whole language program in your classroom. Use them! They can form the basis of thematic units you will gradually develop.

Small Groups Are A Sin. Nonsense. Common sense tells us that some concepts are better taught in small groups. Use different types of grouping and take care that basic students aren't stuck in the same group all of the time. (See chapter 3 on whole group and small group instruction, pages 27-36.)

No Basals Or Workbooks Allowed. This isn't true. As long as literature and other meaningful reading and writing experiences are included, they can add to your program. (See chapter 2 on basals and workbooks, pages 19-26.)

Kids Are Out Of Control. Absolutely not. They are very busy doing their reading and writing, working in their small groups, and preparing their puppet shows and dioramas to share with the class.

No Skills Are Taught. No! Skills are an important part of a whole language program. The only difference is that skills are no longer taught in isolation; they become part of the daily reading, writing, listening, and speaking process.

It Involves Too Much Work For Teachers. Definitely not—it's merely different. Once the adjustment is made, teaching thematic units actually makes planning easier. Teachers, students, and parents realize that all activities and instruction fit together in ways never seen before.

Chapter Two

WHAT HAPPENS TO BASALS, WORKBOOKS, AND SEATWORK?

What happens to basals, workbooks, and seatwork in a whole language program? Nothing—as long as they do not drive the curriculum. When used sparingly and with purpose, basals and workbooks do have a place in the whole language classroom. In the past, basal reading programs were bland and watered down; the stories they provided did little to excite students and made reading a drudgery. Now that the major commercial reading programs include a vast array of literature, basals aren't as limited as they once were. The teacher's manuals accompanying these programs also recommend a number of excellent whole language activities which employ a great deal of listening, speaking, reading, and writing skills.

HOW TO USE BASALS AND WORKBOOKS

The stories in a basal reading series are most helpful with reading groups. It is important to choose stories that can be easily integrated with the units you are already teaching and to select workbook pages that require higher-level thinking. In general, omit any circle-the-answer or fill-in-the-blank responses.

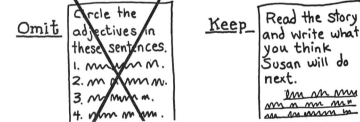

These kinds of responses require little thinking and don't apply the knowledge that students have learned. They constitute nothing more than busy work and have little or no meaning for the learner.

Workbooks typically ask students to either...

circle the item,

cross out what doesn't belong,

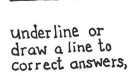

underline or draw a line to correct answers,

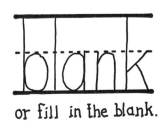

or fill in the blank.

19

Children learn and retain information best by employing the natural learning process of receiving information, processing it, then expressing the information they have learned in real and meaningful ways. A whole language approach allows for this method of learning. The traditional basal or workbook approach does not.

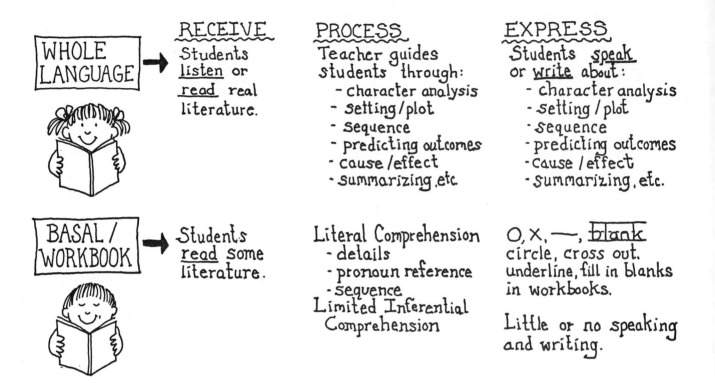

Whole language instruction employs all the modalities of language while the traditional basal or workbook approach employs only some of them. The greatest difference between the two approaches is that the teacher acts as the driving force behind the whole language program, while the workbook or basal approach uses the material as its only impetus.

SEATWORK: WORKBOOKS AND ALTERNATIVES

Seatwork is a necessity if a teacher needs to work on specific skills with small groups of students, for the rest of the class must be engaged in meaningful learning activities that reinforce and apply their knowledge. Because of this, the quality of the seatwork is crucial. The best rules to follow when selecting workbook pages or reproducible worksheets for students to complete on their own are to:

• OMIT activities which ask students to circle correct answers, cross out answers that don't belong, underline or draw a line to correct answers, or fill in a blank.

- KEEP pages which ask students to think about what they read, then

- EXTEND worksheets to allow students to apply their knowledge.

Alternatives to worksheets and workbooks are even better, for they free students to express their knowledge in a variety of meaningful ways.

SEATWORK AND ALTERNATIVES FOR EMERGENT LEARNERS (Grades K-1)

As emergent learners are just becoming aware of the basic skills involved in reading and writing, much of their seatwork activities will entail drawing pictures, cutting and pasting, copying from the board, and the most basic of written responses. Here are some examples of types of worksheets to omit and their possible alternatives, worksheets to keep and extend, and other activities.

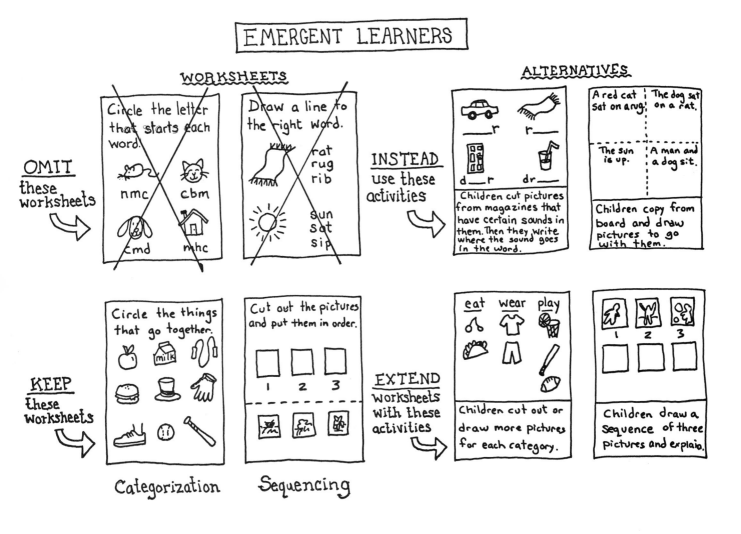

Other Activities: All of these activities employ whole concepts and reinforce many of the important reading skills outlined on the Scope and Sequence Chart of Whole Language Skills (pages 16-17).

"Read" Wordless Books

Children relate story to a partner or an adult.

Puppets

Act out a story with puppets.

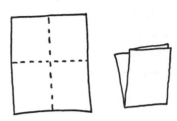

Fold Books

Draw/write a story. Read it to a friend.

Listening Post

Listen and follow along with a favorite story.

Pocket Chart

Arrange words and phrases of predictable books in pocket chart.

Poster

Draw or cut out magazine pictures relating to a topic being studied.

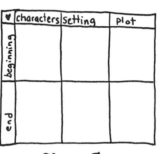

Story Frame

Draw/write characters, setting, plot of story. (NOTE: start with character and setting first.)

Act It Out

Act out favorite stories using cut out faces.

Flipbooks

Draw and write beginning and end of story. (NOTE: encourage invented spelling.)

Categorize Pictures

Categorize laminated pictures of story characters or animals studied. Encourage children to categorize in as many ways as possible.

Box It or Bag It

Collect objects/pictures having to do with concept being studied:
- letter sounds
- shapes
- plants
- animals, etc.

Children share with a partner or adult.

Shape Books

Draw/write a story about whatever shape the book is. Read it to a partner or adult. (NOTE: encourage invented spelling.)

Developing learners have mastered basic reading and writing skills. Their instruction should involve exercises that help them gain deeper meaning from their reading and extend their writing experiences.

Below are some examples of the types of worksheets to omit and their possible alternatives. Also included are examples of worksheets to keep, how to extend them, and additional activities.

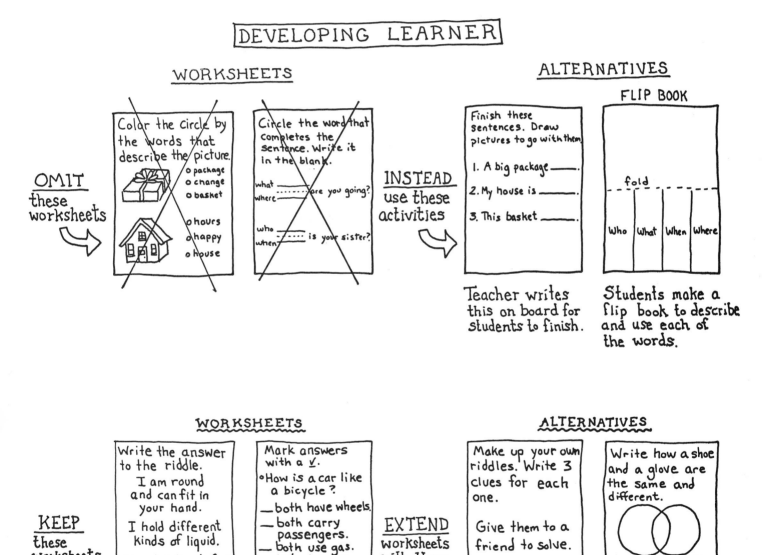

DEVELOPING LEARNER

WORKSHEETS   ALTERNATIVES

FLIP BOOK

OMIT these worksheets

Color the circle by the words that describe the picture.
o package
o change
o basket
o hours
o happy
o house

Circle the word that completes the sentence. Write it in the blank.
what _____
where _____ are you going?
who _____
when _____ is your sister?

INSTEAD use these activities

Finish these sentences. Draw pictures to go with them.
1. A big package _____.
2. My house is _____.
3. This basket _____.

Teacher writes this on board for students to finish.

fold
Who | What | When | Where

Students make a flip book to describe and use each of the words.

WORKSHEETS   ALTERNATIVES

KEEP these worksheets

Write the answer to the riddle.
I am round and can fit in your hand.
I hold different kinds of liquid.
You drink out of me. What am I?
- - - - - - - - -

INFERENTIAL COMPREHENSION

Mark answers with a ✓.
○ How is a car like a bicycle?
___ both have wheels.
___ both carry passengers.
___ both use gas.
___ kids drive them.
○ How is a shoe like a glove?

COMPARE/CONTRAST

EXTEND worksheets with these activities

Make up your own riddles. Write 3 clues for each one.

Give them to a friend to solve.

Write how a shoe and a glove are the same and different.

·SHOE· ·GLOVE·

Make up another comparison.

23

Other Activities: All of these activities utilize whole concepts and engage all the modalities of whole language—listening, speaking, reading, and writing.

Character Conversation
Write cartoons of story characters and their dialogue.

Rewrite the Story
Rewrite story with changes in it.

ABC Book
Write an entry for every letter about a subject or story studied.

Story Frame
Write and draw the characters, setting, and plot for the beginning, middle, and end of story.

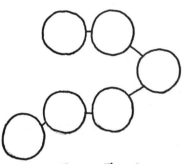

Chain Events
Write and draw the sequence of events in a story.

Puppets
Act out stories with puppets.

Triarama
Color and cut/paste a scene from a story or subject being studied.

Story Project
Make or do something mentioned in the story.

Shape Books
Cut out books in distinctive shapes to write original stories or summaries of books read.

Response Log
Draw, write, tell, or act out reactions to story, characters, or events and tell why.

Act It Out
Act out events of a story or dramatize important aspects of the unit being studied.

Long Tale
Write and draw major story events on a length of shelf paper, such as:
- character
- problem
- solution.

Fluent learners have fully mastered reading and writing skills. Their instruction should be focused on activities which promote their critical thinking abilities and help them to develop strategies appropriate for the types of reading they are doing.

Examples of worksheets to omit, keep, and extend, as well as additional activities, are outlined below.

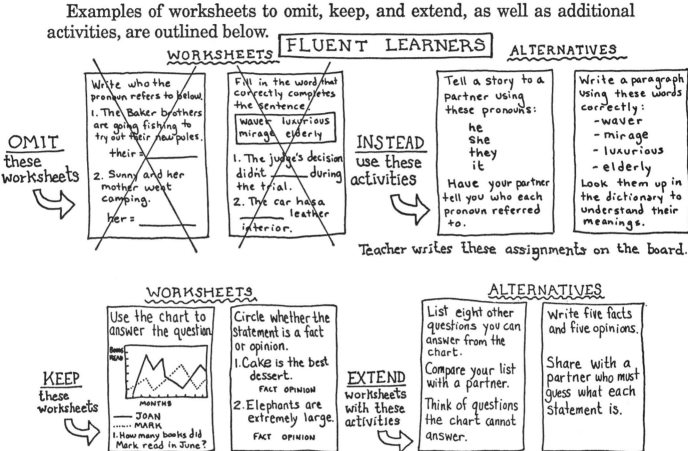

FLUENT LEARNERS

WORKSHEETS

OMIT these worksheets

Write who the pronoun refers to below.
1. The Baker brothers are going fishing to try out their new poles.
   their =
2. Sunny and her mother went camping.
   her =

Fill in the word that correctly completes the sentence.
waver luxurious mirage elderly
1. The judge's decision didn't _____ during the trial.
2. The car has a _____ leather interior.

ALTERNATIVES

INSTEAD use these activities

Tell a story to a partner using these pronouns:
he
she
they
it
Have your partner tell you who each pronoun referred to.

Write a paragraph using these words correctly:
- waver
- mirage
- luxurious
- elderly
Look them up in the dictionary to understand their meanings.

Teacher writes these assignments on the board.

WORKSHEETS

KEEP these worksheets

Use the chart to answer the question
BOOKS READ
MONTHS
—— JOAN
······ MARK
1. How many books did Mark read in June?

MAPS/CHARTS

Circle whether the statement is a fact or opinion.
1. Cake is the best dessert.
   FACT OPINION
2. Elephants are extremely large.
   FACT OPINION

FACT/OPINION

ALTERNATIVES

EXTEND worksheets with these activities

List eight other questions you can answer from the chart.
Compare your list with a partner.
Think of questions the chart cannot answer.

Write five facts and five opinions.
Share with a partner who must guess what each statement is.

Other Activities: All of these exercises require advanced thinking skills and promote the skills areas listed on the Scope and Sequence Chart of Whole Language Skills (pages 16-17). They also employ all of the modalities of whole language—listening, speaking, reading, and writing.

Character Portrayal
Dress up as a character in the story. Explain what happened to you.

Chain Story Events
Chain events of story if a major aspect were changed.

Book Jacket
Design a book jacket with cover, plot summary, and author biography.

Flip Book
Write and draw about a story's character, problem, and solution.

Rewrite Ending
Rewrite the ending of a book or story. Illustrate it.

Character Caddy
Draw, write, collect things the characters might have in their purses or pockets. Explain your choices using evidence from the story.

Poster
Design a poster advertising the book, character, or author.

Venn Diagram
Illustrate similarities and differences between characters or stories.

Triarama
Color, cut, and paste a scene from a book or subject being studied.

About the Author
Write a biography of the author of the book - or - tell about the author in first person.

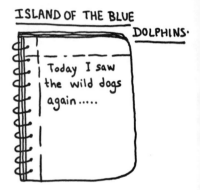

Character Dialog
Draw cartoons of the story and dialog between characters.

Character Diary
Write a diary of one of the characters in the story.

Retell Story on Tape
Retell story complete with sound effects and voice inflection. This can also be done from the main character's point of view.

Poetry
Tell about a character or summarize story in the form of a poem.

Story Frame
Complete a story frame of characters, setting, and plot for beginning, middle, and end of story.

Response Journal
Summarize a chapter and respond to the characters and plot.

Chapter Three

SMALL GROUP vs. WHOLE GROUP INSTRUCTION

Students benefit from a variety of grouping situations, both homogeneous and heterogeneous; therefore, both whole groups and small groups have a place in the whole language classroom. Unfortunately, there are some educators who feel that teaching in small homogeneous groups is the wrong approach. They make the assumption that small group instruction is somehow harmful to students and, therefore, that all teaching should be done in a whole group set-up. Common sense and educational research tell us otherwise. For example, stop and think about your own experiences as a student. Remember sitting in a large lecture hall, and then remember your small seminar. In most cases, you received more personalized attention in the small group and were likely to ask more questions and interact more frequently with the teacher and students there. The large group, however, was a perfect place for the teacher to introduce and explain a new concept as it provided an opportunity to absorb the new information, think about that information, and practice it in order to formulate questions to ask later in a small group format.

Both large and small group situations, then, are necessary for well-rounded instruction. Although this idea may seem clear enough, the concept of small group learning has been misinterpreted by many advocates of whole language. This was a puzzle to me, so I dug into the research which the report *Becoming a Nation of Readers* cited on the subject. The researchers reported that:

- Low-ability groups spend too much time on word lists, flashcards, and decoding skills applied out of context.
- Those in low-ability reading groups often feel stigmatized and consider themselves poor readers. (Teachers also have lower expectations of them.)
- Children rarely move from one reading group to another.

The conclusion, then, isn't that small groups are wrong, but rather that care should be taken to bring real meaning to instruction, small group make-up should be varied often to avoid stigma, and frequent "visits" by students to other groups should be encouraged. Groups should also be kept flexible in order that students not feel chained to the same batch of kids.

FLEXIBLE GROUPING (SMALL GROUP INSTRUCTION)

Flexible grouping is an important aspect of any good whole language program. It keeps students from feeling stigmatized, helps them develop necessary skills and concepts, and gives them experience working constructively with other students. Flexible small groups can be arranged by:

- Skills/Concept Review
- Pairs
- Invitation
- Cooperative
- Interest
- Numbers (Heterogeneous)
- Ability Level (Homogeneous)

Skills/Concept Review: This type of group should be formed when an informal assessment reveals that some students are having trouble with a particular concept. (For more information, see Chapter 10–Evaluation, pages 120-133.) This assessment can be made by evaluating the class's writing to determine who understands that concept and who doesn't. Those students who do not understand the required concept can be called together for review. They should then be provided with practice exercises which allow them to apply their knowledge in meaningful ways.

Example: After a class exercise of writing thank-you letters, a few students still don't understand letter form. The teacher discreetly invites them to help with another letter-writing activity.

Teacher models writing student-dictated letter, instructing on correct letter form.

Depending on ability level, students either copy letter or write their own.

This same approach can be applied to virtually all skills and concepts with students of all ages. Furthermore, it doesn't stigmatize the students; it engages them in a real learning situation which is what whole language is all about!

Pairs: Two students can be paired to read together. They can be grouped together in one of three ways: one of high ability and one of low ability, both students with equal ability, or students can choose their own reading buddies. All of these pairings have equal validity and can be used at different times.

The high-/low-ability pairing is helpful to the low-ability student because the high-ability student provides a good model for reading fluency and developing vocabulary and listening skills. This type of grouping also helps the high-ability student as it provides practice working with another student and reading a favorite book aloud.

Pairs of equal-ability students can take turns reading to each other from the same book. Through this type of grouping, they gain practice reading aloud and develop confidence about their reading.

Reading buddies chosen by the students themselves can share their favorite books with their partners. They can discuss them, read aloud their favorite parts, and point out favorite pictures.

High/Low Pair

High-ability student reads aloud to low-ability student. This models fluency.

Equal-Ability Pairs

Read to one another out of the same book. This bolsters fluency and self-confidence.

Reading Buddies

Share favorite books with one another. Discuss favorite parts/pictures, etc.

Invitation: By keeping an open invitation for students to visit other groups, everyone benefits. Periodic invitations by the teacher for individuals, pairs, or entire groups of children to sit in on another group and participate in the lesson have proven tremendously successful. Teachers can make an open invitation to all those interested in attending, or plan for specific groups to visit other groups.

Everyone wins this way. Students become active partners in their own education, their self-esteem is bolstered, and teachers can present an extended lesson to a combined group. This cuts planning time in half!

I will be reading *Charlotte's Web* with the Red Reading Group. Anyone who would like to listen and read along is invited.

OPEN INVITATION

Children choose if they want to visit or not.

Today the Red and Blue groups will meet and discuss *Sarah, Plain and Tall*. Paired reading will be one Red and one Blue member.

SPECIFIC INVITATION

Teacher directs the visitation of specific students / groups.

Cooperative: The concept behind cooperative grouping is simple—students work together to complete a specific task. No elaborate set-up is necessary. Simply arrange students in groups of three or four (the teacher can do this, or the students can themselves) and have groups work together on tasks involving teamwork. These can include:

- brainstorming ideas and recording them
- science, math, and social studies concepts/projects
- performing a play or puppet show
- working on games and puzzles.

Do not immediately expect these groups to cooperate fully and work together. Group work is a separate skill, and students need time to effectively learn it. Emergent learners will need special help easing into cooperative activities since their interactive skills are still being developed. Developing and fluent learners can be given more complicated tasks as they will have had more experience working in groups.

Think about what you will write. Tell a partner, then do your work.

Emergent Learners

Begin working with just one partner to practice concept.

In your group, choose other things Frederick could collect from Summer. Write a group list.

BBQ Smell! I'll write I'll Draw

Developing Learners

Group brainstorms and lists ideas.

Imagine you are a pioneer coming West. Write about who you are, where you are going. Keep a journal and draw a map of your journey.

Fluent Learners

Group develops ideas into full projects.

Interest: Another way to group students is according to interest. Interest groups allow for great flexibility and provide students with a sense of self-control as they participate in forming their own groups. It also encourages the skills needed for cooperative groups. The teacher provides three to five activities and students choose to complete the ones that interest them. These can be daily activity choices or reserved for specific days of the week. (Tuesdays and Thursdays can be set aside for these activities, for example, or you may want to institute "Fun Fridays.")

INVOLVES READING

Reread story and act it out.

INVOLVES SPEAKING

Listen to your favorite stories.

INVOLVES LISTENING

INVOLVES WRITING

Draw and write a billboard for this book.

It is a good idea to offer choices involving all aspects of whole language. Small area rugs, bath mats, and tables are excellent means for limiting group size. Students have to choose another activity if one is full.

Numbers: This type of grouping provides a terrific arbitrary way to call up a heterogeneous group. Simply assign each student a number from one to five which he or she will keep for the entire year. When working on such projects as a science or social studies folder, creative stories, or researching a particular subject, the teacher calls up all the 2's, for example, and works with them.

Ability Level: There is nothing wrong with occasionally grouping by ability level. Make sure, however, that students are not locked into this type of grouping and are involved in stimulating lessons, as well. (See Chapter 5–Presenting A Perfect Lesson, pages 42-45.) In fact, studies have shown that high-ability children often benefit from homogeneous ability grouping. The best rule to consider when placing children in homogeneous groups is to re-examine and change the groups every six weeks. With this method, no child runs the risk of feeling stigmatized.

There should be a healthy balance between whole group and small group instruction. A whole language program is far from being a one-size-fits-all approach to learning. Many aspects of reading, writing, listening, speaking, and the thematic units that incorporate these skills easily lend themselves to whole groups.

You can assemble the whole group to:
- begin the school day, make announcements, review the calendar, etc.
- read a story
- facilitate discussion
- encourage class sharing
- oversee response journals
- introduce a new concept
- watch a performance (student play, puppet show, film/video, guest speakers).

The most important guidelines to follow when forming groups are to use a common-sense approach and group according to a given situation.

A TYPICAL WHOLE LANGUAGE DAY

Keep in mind that certain subjects and situations are best suited for particular types of groups. By allowing the situation to dictate the types of groups formed and by keeping groups flexible, students will be exposed to a variety of stimulating learning environments.

Three examples of a typical whole language day follow, one each for emergent, developing, and fluent learners. Each example considers the skills and ability levels of the children and offers a number of grouping arrangements, but occasionally has children working independently, as well.

SAMPLE DAY FOR EMERGENT LEARNERS (Grades K-1)

Emergent learners are becoming aware of the basics of reading and writing, and much of their day is spent listening to various stories and completing speaking, pre-reading, and writing activities based on those stories. (For more specifics on these types of activities, see Chapter 6–Listening and Speaking, Chapter 7–Reading and Comprehension, and Chapter 8–Writing.)

NOTE: Initials stand for the following:

(WG) ....Whole Group	(HG) ....Heterogeneous Group
(I) ....Independent	(IG) ....Interest Group
(AG) ....Ability [Homogeneous] Group	(CG)..........................Cooperative Group
(P)..................................Pairs	

WG: OPENING (10-15 min) - Roll call, lunch count, calendar, seasonal songs, and fingerplays. (Some can be written on charts which the class follows as the teacher or a child points to the words.)

READING/LANGUAGE ARTS (90 min)

(WG) 15 min. Teacher reads aloud.

(I) 10-15 min. Journal writing. Students draw pictures about events in a story and dictate or write invented spelling stories.

(AG) 60 min. Reading Group Rotation

Group 1	Group 2	Group 3
Skills lesson from read-aloud book	Arrange pocket chart words	Listening post

RECESS

MATH (30 minutes)

(CG) 15 min. Teacher models patterning geometric shapes on board. Cooperative Groups complete patterns on chalkboards.

(I,P) 15 min. Students complete patterning worksheets, then draw their own patterns for partners to complete.

IG: CHOICES (15-30 minutes)

Students choose from these activities:

- reading games
- art center (draw cover of favorite book)
- performance area (act out a story)
- library
- writing center (make a fold book)

LUNCH

WG: READ ALOUD (20 minutes) Teacher reads aloud.

WG: SCIENCE/SOCIAL STUDIES/ART/MUSIC (60 minutes)

Students view films, participate in science experiments, graphing, map studies, singing, etc.

RECESS

I: SUSTAINED SILENT READING (10-20 minutes)

Students choose a few books, find comfortable places to sit, and read or look at their books.

HG: PHYSICAL EDUCATION (20 minutes)

Teacher forms heterogeneous groups and numbers them for these activities:

Group 1	Group 2	Group 3	Group 4
Ball Skills	Jump Rope	Balance Beam	Follow-the-leader

WG: CULMINATING ACTIVITIES

DISMISSAL

SAMPLE DAY FOR DEVELOPING LEARNERS (Grades 2-3)

Developing learners have already gained basic reading and writing skills and can understand the material they read. These students are capable of more independent work than are emergent learners, and that fact is taken into consideration in the group activities of this sample day. For more specific activities, see Chapter 6–Listening and Speaking, Chapter 7–Reading and Comprehension, and Chapter 8–Writing.

NOTE: Initials stand for the following:

(WG) ....Whole Group
(I) ....Independent
(AG) ....Ability [Homogeneous] Group
(P)...Pairs

(HG) ....Heterogeneous Group
(IG) ....Interest Group
(CG)...............................Cooperative Group
(BI) ....By Invitation

WG: OPENING (10-15 min) - Roll call, lunch count, calendar, class news, current events.
READING/LANGUAGE ARTS (90 min)
(WG) 15 minutes: Teacher reads aloud.
(I) 15 minutes: Journal writing. Children write and draw pictures about aspects of the story the teacher read. Invented spelling is still accepted.
(AG, P) 60 minutes: Reading Group Rotation

Group 1	Group 2	Group 3
Skills lesson from literature book	Paired reading	Students copy board-work and illustrate it

RECESS
MATH (45 minutes)
(WG) Teacher explains the concept of measurement by the inch.
(CG) Cooperative groups measure items to complete a worksheet, then extend it with other measurements.
CHOICES (15-30 minutes)
(IG)   Children choose from these activities:
   • writing center (shape book)
   • library
   • listening center.
(BI) Teacher shows one reading group how to construct a triarama and invites other interested groups to join in.
LUNCH

WG: READ ALOUD (20 minutes) Teacher reads aloud.
SCIENCE/SOCIAL STUDIES/ART/MUSIC (60 minutes)
(WG) Teacher introduces the four food groups.
(HG) Class is divided into four heterogeneous groups, one for each food group. Each group cuts pictures of their food groups from magazines and pastes them on a poster.
RECESS

I: SUSTAINED SILENT READING (15-25 minutes)
Children choose a few books or take their library books, find comfortable places to sit, and read quietly.

HG: PHYSICAL EDUCATION (20 minutes)
Relays between heterogeneous teams.

WG: CULMINATING ACTIVITIES
DISMISSAL

SAMPLE DAY FOR FLUENT LEARNERS (Grades 4-6)

Fluent learners have mastered the basics of reading and writing; therefore, they should concentrate on developing strategies for reading and comprehending more advanced story elements such as an author's intent and mood.

NOTE: Initials stand for the following:

(WG)..............................Whole Group	(P)..Pairs	(CG).........Cooperative Group
(I)......................................Independent	(HG)....Heterogeneous Group	(BI)....................By Invitation
(AG)....Ability [Homogeneous] Group	(IG)................Interest Group	(SCR)...Skill/Concept Review

WG: OPENING (10-15 min) - Roll call, lunch count, announcements, current events.
READING/LANGUAGE ARTS (90 min)
(WG) 15 minutes: Teacher reads aloud.
(I) 15 minutes: Journal Writing. Students write and draw their responses to the material the teacher read.
(AG, P)   60 minutes: Reading Group Rotation

Group 1	Group 2	Group 3
Skills lesson from literature book	Venn diagram comparing characters	Story frame cause/ effect relationship

RECESS
MATH (60 minutes)
(WG) Teacher reviews concepts of multiplying with regrouping.
(I) Independently, students complete board problems.
(SCR) Teacher works with small group of students who are having trouble with the concept.
FORMAL WRITING (15-30 minutes)
(WG) Teacher introduces the concept of organizing information by semantic mapping to write paragraphs.
(CG)   Cooperative groups brainstorm and collectively write a paragraph from the semantic map.
LUNCH

WG: READ ALOUD (20 minutes) Teacher reads aloud.
SCIENCE/SOCIAL STUDIES/ART/MUSIC (60 minutes)
(WG) Teacher discusses trails pioneers took in covered wagons. Introduces map.
(HG) Groups brainstorm all information they can and cannot glean from the map. They make a list of questions about pioneers, then brainstorm where they can find the answers.
RECESS

I: SUSTAINED SILENT READING (25-30 minutes)
Students choose books to read, find comfortable places to sit, and read their books quietly.

HG: PHYSICAL EDUCATION (20 minutes)
Square dancing.

WG: CULMINATING ACTIVITIES
DISMISSAL

Notice that the developing and fluent learners are involved in activities using higher-level thinking skills which have no right or wrong answers. It is the students' thinking processes that matter, not simply the end product.

The best rule of thumb for grouping in a whole language classroom is to consistently change group make-up. Keep groups flexible and change according to need. From pairs and cooperative groups to ability grouping and whole group instruction, all group formats have a place in a well-rounded program.

Chapter Four

SETTING UP THE CLASSROOM

A few basic classroom elements should remain the same from kindergarten through the sixth grade:

- Students are surrounded with print.
- Areas are designated for purposeful work.
- Students assume responsibility for their own learning.

In this chapter, each of these elements is explored in depth in order to make clear the framework of a good whole language classroom.

STUDENTS ARE SURROUNDED WITH PRINT

Students of all ages and ability levels should be surrounded with books and writing of all kinds. Classroom walls, doors, desks, cabinets, and learning centers can be covered with student work. Writing samples, charts and graphs, and thematic projects should replace commercial and teacher-made bulletin boards. Student-made posters, mobiles, and other art projects can hang from the ceiling or can be suspended from a clothesline strung across the room. Displaying student work in this manner is important because children refer to and learn from material they have made themselves. A print-dominated room also models the idea that reading and writing are life skills.

In addition to books and student work, maps, globes, charts, and graphs should be prominent in the classroom, and many references should be made to these tools throughout the school day.

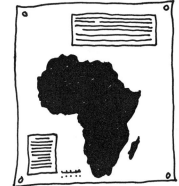

Every whole language classroom needs these basic student work stations:
- Class library
- Listening center
- Art or project area
- Writing center
- Large group area

Daily activities should be planned for these areas; students can be asked to rotate from the various work stations, be assigned to a particular work station upon completing an assignment, or be assigned to one of the areas for seatwork.

Class Library: The class library should be an inviting area decorated with bookshelves and comfortable chairs, pillows, and other interesting places for students to relax and read. In addition to numerous books, there should be magazines, maps, newspapers, menus, recipes, books the class has made, and any other reading material the students may enjoy. A variety of reading material reinforces the concept of reading as a life skill.

Some magazines appropriate for elementary students are:
- *Sesame Street* (grades K-1)
- *Your Big Backyard* (grades K-2)
- *Ranger Rick* (grades K-3)
- *Highlights for Children* (grades 1-3)
- *Sports Illustrated for Kids* (grades 2-6)
- *National Geographic World* (grades 2-6)
- *Penny Power* (grades 2-6)
- *3-2-1 Contact* (grades 2-6)

Arrange magazines, big books, and newspapers on racks, and periodically categorize books by author or subject to give students experience with organizational patterns.

There should be enough copies of books for paired reading, reading groups, and take-home reading.

Listening Center: Every kindergarten through sixth grade classroom should have a listening center equipped with headsets; students can listen to tapes or stories while following along in the books. Older students can record stories they have written and make up commercials for products they have designed on paper. Class radio programs can be designed in small groups and recorded. Music, mystery sounds, and directions to follow should also be included.

The possibilities of a listening center for both young children and older students are limitless!

Listen to stories and follow along (older students could make recordings for younger children).

Record commercials and radio programs students have written.

Listen to music.

Identify mystery sounds.

Art or Project Area: Creativity is an important aspect of the whole language program. When students have free time or are given a follow-up assignment after a lesson, material should be available for them to work on creative projects.

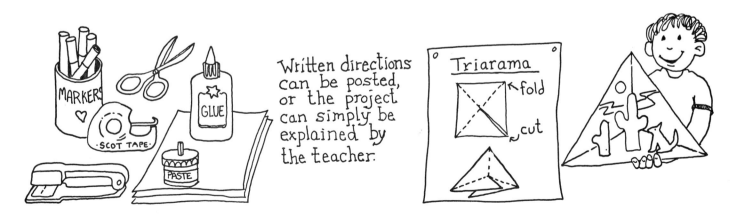

Written directions can be posted, or the project can simply be explained by the teacher.

Writing Center: The writing center should have many different kinds of paper on which students can write. It may also have a typewriter, rubber stamps, envelopes, codes, and any other tools related to writing. The idea is to reinforce the notion that reading is a life skill by offering students a number of writing situations.

File for Ideas

Shape Books

Lengths of white shelf paper

Teeny Tiny Books

Write in code

Individual Chalkboards w/chalk & sock eraser.

Large Group Area: The large group area is a space for the entire class to gather for singing, movement, stories, and other informal whole group activities. It also provides a place for student puppet shows and plays to be performed.

STUDENTS ASSUME RESPONSIBILITY FOR THEIR LEARNING

In a whole language classroom the students are able to assume some of the responsibilities that belong only to the teacher in a traditional program. This provides students with opportunities to make choices about the books and activities on which they will work. Discipline is not disregarded, however. Students are merely responsible for their own behavior. When their assigned work is completed, they can choose from a number of options available at the centers and project areas discussed.

PUTTING IT ALL TOGETHER

When all of these aspects of a whole language program are implemented, the classroom takes on a busy hum of activity as the students become immersed in their learning.

Chapter Five

PRESENTING A PERFECT LESSON

Research into the learning and retention process reveals that there are some common denominators which dramatically affect a student's learning process. They are:
- Pre-lesson activities
- Direction during the lesson
- Follow-up activities

These activities need not be elaborate or involve large amounts of planning time. Their purpose is to make students feel connected to the learning by relating concepts to the students' own experiences. They are so simple to implement, yet make all the difference in the world. When concepts that are developed during the lesson are reinforced with meaningful activities after the lesson, the learning is complete.

PRE-LESSON ACTIVITY

Students don't automatically make the connection between their own experiences and information they read. As a result, they often fail to retain information they have read because the bits of information have no real meaning to them.

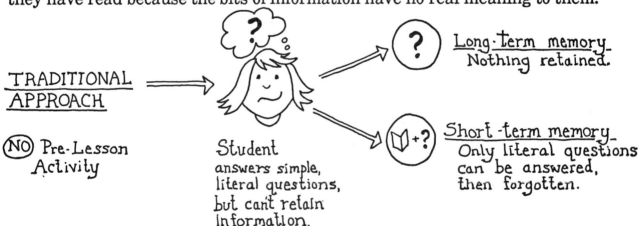

TRADITIONAL APPROACH

(NO) Pre-Lesson Activity

Student answers simple, literal questions, but can't retain information.

? Long-term memory. Nothing retained.

+? Short-term memory. Only literal questions can be answered, then forgotten.

Without a pre-lesson activity, critical thinking or inferential comprehension is impossible because the students have no personal knowledge on which to draw. It is the teacher's job, then, to connect the students' own experiences to the learning.

When this is done, the students not only retain the information, they can utilize higher-level thinking skills to assess it, as well. Since thinking underlies all education, pre-lesson activities are essential to any real learning.

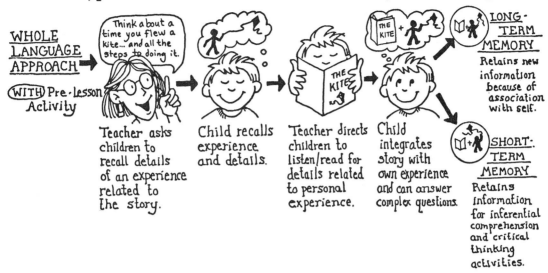

The only way students can retain information they have learned in their long-term memories is to form an association with something meaningful and personal to them. By doing so they are also able to process more complex information and discuss concepts requiring critical thinking and inferential comprehension.

The pre-lesson activity can be presented in a number of ways:
- Asking students to *think* about their experiences
- *Discussing* their knowledge and experiences
- *Writing/Mapping* their knowledge and ideas on the board

After completing the pre-lesson activity, the teacher should always direct the students to listen to or read the story for a specific purpose. This technique also dramatically increases comprehension.

THINK   DISCUSSION   MAPPING

DIRECTION DURING THE LESSON

The next step in presenting a perfect lesson is to direct the learning during the lesson. This is done by simply stopping periodically and asking some

43

thought-provoking questions that reinforce literal, inferential, and critical thinking skills. Some of these questions might include:

- **Drawing Conclusions:** "What do you think the character will do next?" "Why?"
- **Predicting Outcomes:** "How do you think the story will end?" "Why?"
- **Details & Compare/Contrast:** "Think about zoo animals you know and the ones you have read about. How are they the same or different?"
- **Analyzing Characters:** "Think about why the character is doing this."

While the teacher must take care not to interrupt the flow of the story too many times, stopping periodically to direct students' attention enhances the learning experience. Learning can be further enhanced by a related follow-up activity.

FOLLOW-UP ACTIVITY

These activities reinforce in students the learning established in the pre-lesson activity and developed during the lesson. It is important for these activities to be real applications of the students' learning and not fragmented responses marked on traditional worksheets.

Whole language means dealing with whole concepts. When students apply their knowledge in meaningful ways, they are engaging a number of concepts and thinking processes to complete the required task. Good follow-up activities for the pre-lesson activities previously cited include:

After discussion, and the teacher has written ideas on board, students make a flipbook.

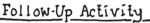

After discussion, and teacher has written ideas on board, students chain ideas by drawing/writing their own chains.

Teacher circles animals and what they eat from student responses after the reading. Students mention other animals/food from story. Students then write sentences about animals from information on board.

44

Once the students have become accustomed to these activities, they can be used as seatwork exercises both before and after the teacher meets with small groups for instruction. This technique works best with developing and fluent learners who have already developed more sophisticated reading and writing skills.

	Developing	Fluent
Group 1:	Draw something you are afraid of. Draw and write what you do when you are afraid. We will read *Harry and the Terrible Whatzit*.	List things you would pack if you were going to live in the woods. Then, skim chapters 1-2 in *My Side of the Mountain* for the things that Sam took with him.
Group 2:	Draw and write your favorite things about summer. Bring them to the group. We will read *Frederick* today.	Make a Venn diagram comparing yourself to Shirley in *In The Year of the Boar and Jackie Robinson*.
Group 3:	Write three questions you would want to have answered about someone you haven't met. Bring them to the group. We'll be starting *Sarah, Plain and Tall* today.	Design a special place for yourself. What would you name it? Skim chapter 4 of *Bridge to Terabithia* for Jess and Leslie's imaginary place. Think how your imaginary place is similar to or different from theirs. Be prepared to discuss in a group.

These aspects of good lesson design can be implemented in virtually all lessons presented in the areas of math, science, social studies, etc.

Chapter Six

LISTENING AND SPEAKING

Listening and speaking skills are vital to the successful reception and expression of information; therefore, activities which promote listening and speaking skills are important components of the whole language program.

Unfortunately, the older students become, the less they are exposed to activities which develop these vital skills. While they may seem simple and are easily overlooked in the classroom, listening and speaking activities are critically important to the reading and writing process. The listening, speaking, reading, and writing processes are all interconnected; each activity adds to and takes from the others. It is this concept which forms the framework of the whole language program, as well as what sets it apart from a traditional learning program. Rather than separate these modalities, whole language introduces these concepts at the same time to enhance the learning process.

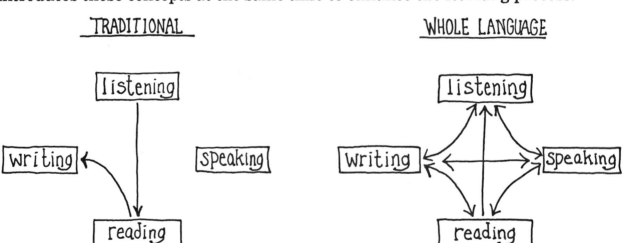

This is the traditional vocabulary/ reader/workbook approach. It engages few of the language modalities and, therefore, is quite limited.

This is a typical whole language lesson that involves a good deal of listening and speaking to enhance reading and writing skills.

We know that the receptive language of young children (the language they hear and understand) is much higher than their expressive language (the language they speak or write). This remains true for both elementary and middle school students in grades K-6. Thus, the best way for these students to increase their knowledge and vocabulary is by listening to a variety of sources that present a variety of concepts. Listed here are a number of listening activities and their appropriate grade levels.

Remember, all students should have daily opportunities to listen.

Grades	K	1	2	3	4	5	6
Stories, poems, and books teacher reads aloud	x	x	x	x	x	x	x
Identify recordings of "mystery sounds"	x	x	x	x	x	x	x
Tapes of stories, songs, and recordings	x	x	x	x	x	x	x
Listening post	x	x	x	x	x	x	x
Sequence of oral directions	x	x	x	x	x	x	x
Plays/puppet shows	x	x	x	x	x	x	x
Class discussion	x	x	x	x	x	x	x
Guest speakers	x	x	x	x	x	x	x
Book talks	x	x	x	x	x	x	x
Paired reading	x	x	x	x	x	x	x

In addition to daily listening opportunities as part of literature-based reading, games and fun-filled activities should be introduced. For example, the teacher can periodically stop other activities to introduce one of these short exercises:

- Have children stop and listen to all the sounds outside and then write them down or draw them.

- Play "Simon Says."

- Follow directions: You might say "When I say 'Go,' you clap your hands twice, stand up, turn around, and sit down." Then review with the children what you will say and what they are to do. First try to fool them by saying something other than "Go"; then say it correctly. This keeps everybody on their toes, and students of all ages enjoy it tremendously.

"Simon Says... pat your tummy."

47

Another method for introducing new concepts and vocabulary words to students is to provide them with many speaking opportunities. The more students hear and comprehend language, the better they will be able to express their own thoughts. Furthermore, it is only after their listening and speaking skills are developed that students begin to translate their learning into the more advanced skills of reading, comprehension, and writing.

A number of speaking activities are listed below with their appropriate grade levels indicated. Students should have meaningful opportunities to speak every day in one-on-one, paired, small group, and large group situations.

Grades	K	1	2	3	4	5	6
Sharing, show-and-tell	x	x	x	x	x	x	x
Class discussion	x	x	x	x	x	x	x
Retell/act-out stories	x	x	x	x	x	x	x
Perform plays	x	x	x	x	x	x	x
Stage a puppet show	x	x	x	x	x	x	x
Sing a song	x	x	x	x	x	x	x
Recite poems and chants	x	x	x	x	x	x	x
Explain an activity or project	x	x	x	x	x	x	x
Brainstorm ideas	x	x	x	x	x	x	x
Paired reading	x	x	x	x	x	x	x
Share a favorite book	x	x	x	x	x	x	x
Record the retelling of a story			x	x	x	x	x
Character portrayals from books			x	x	x	x	x
Reader's theater			x	x	x	x	x
Oral reports				x	x	x	x
Record interviews					x	x	x
Panel/small group discussions						x	x
Debate							x

Listening and speaking activities can be used effectively as seatwork. Students acquire proficiency in reading and writing by experiencing these types of activities:

Listening Post (grades K-6): Students listen to and read along with stories.

Brainstorming Ideas (grades K-6): Students brainstorm and record ideas on a variety of topics: what might happen after the story ends, rewrite the ending, predict what a character will do in a subsequent chapter, etc.

Paired Reading (grades K-6): Students read in pairs.

Retell or Act Out Stories (grades K-6): This activity encourages summarizing and referring to the story for details.

Chapter Seven

READING AND COMPREHENSION

Whole language instruction seeks to extend the natural learning process into the areas of reading comprehension and writing. This can be accomplished most effectively by the teacher asking students to attach personal experiences to their reading, thus increasing their levels of comprehension. Only through such teacher-directed instruction can higher levels of reading comprehension and study skills be obtained.

Daily reading experiences are vital to successful whole language instruction. There are a number of ways to read a text in the classroom:
- Students follow along while the teacher reads aloud.
- Neurological Impress—students read along with the teacher.
- Silent Reading—teacher guides students to read a passage for specific information.
- Paired Reading—students read to each other in pairs.

The reading section of the Scope and Sequence Chart of Whole Language Skills is reproduced on page 51 for reference throughout this chapter.

SCOPE AND SEQUENCE CHART OF WHOLE LANGUAGE SKILLS, K-6

Grades	Emerging		Developing		Fluent		
	K	1	2	3	4	5	6

READING

	K	1	2	3	4	5	6
Teacher Reads Aloud Daily	x	x	x	x	x	x	x
Students Read Silently Every Day	x	x	x	x	x	x	x
Students Read in Other Situations Daily	x	x	x	x	x	x	x
Word Identification							
• phonics (vowels/consonants)	x	x	x				
• contractions, compound words		x	x	x			
• sight words		x	x	x			
Vocabulary							
• recognize word meanings	x	x	x	x	x	x	x
• roots, prefixes, suffixes	x	x	x	x	x	x	x
• synonyms/antonyms	x	x	x	x	x	x	x
• unfamiliar words in context	x	x	x	x	x	x	x
Comprehension							
Literal							
• details	x	x	x	x	x	x	x
• pronoun reference	x	x	x	x	x	x	x
• sequence	x	x	x	x	x	x	x
Inferential							
• relate story to personal experiences	x	x	x	x	x	x	x
• main idea	x	x	x	x	x	x	x
• cause/effect	x	x	x	x	x	x	x
• draw conclusions	x	x	x	x	x	x	x
• predict outcomes	x	x	x	x	x	x	x
• compare/contrast	x	x	x	x	x	x	x
Critical Thinking							
• analyze character, setting	x	x	x	x	x	x	x
• real/make-believe		x	x	x			
• summarize plot			x	x	x	x	x
• fact/opinion					x	x	x
• mood						x	x
• author's tone/intent						x	x
Study Skills							
• maps/charts/graphs	x	x	x	x	x	x	x
• book parts (table of contents/title page/index)	x	x	x	x	x	x	x
• alphabetization			x	x			
• dictionary			x	x	x	x	x
• reference (newspaper/telephone book/ encyclopedia/atlas)			x	x	x	x	x
• card catalog				x	x	x	x

It is important to emphasize inferential comprehension and critical thinking when teaching comprehension skills. All readers must be directed to think about the information they are reading and apply it to their own experiences; otherwise, reading comprehension quickly becomes merely an automatic response to literal questions and lacks depth. To illustrate this point, consider this nonsense passage:

> Mik icked the gik.
> Then he ocked it.
> Last he kacked the gik, and it was zated.

Every question about this passage involving literal comprehension skills can be answered even though the the words themselves make no sense.

Literal Comprehension

Details:
"Who icked the gik?"
(answer: Mik)

"What was icked?"
(answer: the gik)

"What happened to the gik?"
(answer: It was icked and kaked.)

Pronoun Reference:
He = Mik
It = gik

Sequence:
"What happened after Mik icked the gik?"
(answer: It was ocked.)

"What was the last thing that happened in the story?"
(answer: Mik kacked the gik, and it was zated.)

"What happened first?"
(answer: Mik icked the gik.)

This passage provides a perfect example of how low-ability students' comprehension levels can remain unnoticed in traditional reading programs which emphasize literal comprehension. The whole language approach to reading, however, guarantees that students, no matter what their ability level, won't go unnoticed.

EMERGENT LEARNERS (Grades K-1)

Emergent learners have already mastered the ability to listen, understand, and speak language. They are also becoming aware that language can be written and read and are developing the basic skills needed for successful reading and writing. The process they must undergo to become successful readers and writers provides the foundation upon which all later learning will be built. To illustrate the gravity and difficulty of this undertaking, consider this example:

As teachers, we are asking children to decipher a code they may have had little or no experience with.

Ͷ–ΙΙ⅃ ⅃Ͷ–Γ Ͷ⊖Λ–ΙΙ⅃ ⹁Vↄb ⊕–⅃

ↄ⅃ͶͶV ⊖Λ–⅃⅄ ⅃bV 𝄢⅃ ΙΙ–⅃

Deciphered message: "They are being asked to read things like this."

Making sense out of such a code is difficult and illustrates why young children must be given a tremendous amount of experience interacting with print before they can learn to read successfully. It also explains why they must be given all the tools—in the form of letter sounds and phonics—to decipher the code of reading and approximate the pronunciation of each word. Emergent learners must be taught the various elements that make reading understandable before they can begin to read and understand language themselves. While the alphabetic principle is being taught, emergent learners should also be listening to, speaking about, and looking at books, as well as writing and dictating ideas about them.

Each of the reading and comprehension skills for emergent learners listed on the Scope and Sequence Chart of Whole Language Skills (page 51) is analyzed in depth on the following pages (54-64).

Books without words and books with predictable phrases are the most useful for developing emergent learners' reading skills. A list of wordless and predictable books recommended for emergent learners is available in chapter 12 (pages 140-156).

Wordless books allow the teacher to model storytelling from pictures. On their own, the students can repeat this exercise in pairs or during silent reading. Wordless books also encourage students to use picture clues to help them understand story details, character traits, and setting.

TEACHER "READS" WORDLESS BOOKS

PAIRED READING
One child tells about one page, the other tells about the next. They will often use the questioning techniques the teacher has modeled.

CHILD READS SILENTLY

Predictable books are important to emergent learners for the repeated language patterns they present. Children quickly master these patterns and are able to chant along with the teacher. The teacher can best capitalize on this natural process by making available big books with large print and pointing to each word as it is read aloud. After they have mastered chanting with the teacher, students can take turns pointing to the words as they are read.

Exercises involving pocket charts and sentence strips should also be introduced to emergent learners, and these activities work well in conjunction with predictable books. Predictable words and phrases are written on sentence strips and placed in a pocket chart. In small or whole group situations, the students can manipulate the sentence strips then read aloud the sentences or phrases they have created.

Predictable books are read to children who chant along.

Big books allow children to see each word as it is read.

Pocket charts allow children to manipulate and read the predictable phrases they have come to know.

All of these experiences help emergent learners develop the foundation for a sight vocabulary and introduce a variety of comprehension concepts.

It is also important to read aloud picture books to young children. Although picture books may not contain predictable phrases, children need to be exposed to literature beyond their ability to read as this process develops their vocabulary and advanced thinking skills. Remember, children can understand ideas and language far beyond their ability to express them. Always introduce new books and authors to expand young learners' horizons, but return most often to favorite wordless and predictable books.

STUDENTS READ SILENTLY EVERY DAY

A portion of each day should be allotted for silent reading. This is a time for children to choose a few books, find comfortable places in the room to sit, and read quietly. It is crucial for the teacher to read with the students during silent reading time as the teacher is a model for the students' behavior. Young children have short attention spans which can be enhanced with practice. Thus, silent reading units for emergent learners should last for approximately five minutes at the beginning of the year and gradually build to approximately fifteen minutes in duration.

Although emergent readers have not mastered the basics of formalized reading, they can still profit from a number of different reading situations.

Shared Reading
Teacher shares a book by pointing out the author/illustrator, discusses the book during and after it is read, then follows up with an appropriate activity.

Paired Reading
Pairs of children are grouped for reading:
- higher-ability students read to younger ones.
- equal-ability students take turns reading or telling about a favorite book.
- students choose a buddy to read with.

Author Information
Teacher introduces an author's work, talks about his or her background, and the other books and subjects he or she writes about. Students browse through books afterward.

Listening Post
Students listen to taped story and follow along in the book.

Word identification is a crucial skill for emergent readers to develop as they must have every skill available to them to unlock the meanings of words. This is done by first teaching them the alphabetic principle.

Alphabetic principle (phonics):

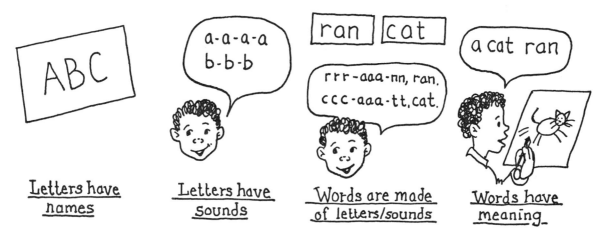

Letters have names   Letters have sounds   Words are made of letters/sounds   Words have meaning

Phonics must be taught in order that children have all the tools at their disposal to approximate the pronunciation of words. Phonics instruction should be kept simple, however, and taught to children at an early age. Because of this, the first selections children read should be consistent with the phonics rules they have learned, and be interesting and understandable. Striking this balance isn't as difficult as it may first seem. One way to do this is to utilize pocket charts, meaningful worksheets, and board work.

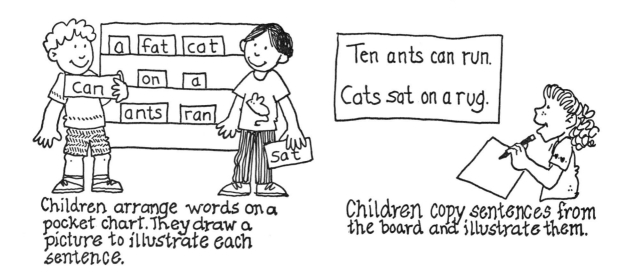

Children arrange words on a pocket chart. They draw a picture to illustrate each sentence.

Children copy sentences from the board and illustrate them.

Always remind children to read for meaning, not simply sound out words.

Contractions and compound words are best taught using the same method as phonics instruction. The teacher first defines a contraction or a compound word and then gives the students meaningful reading experiences with which to apply their knowledge. Contractions and compound words should not be taught simultaneously, however, for young children can internalize only one major concept at a time and need to have experience applying one concept before moving on to a new one.

Sight words should also be taught using pocket charts and chart stories.

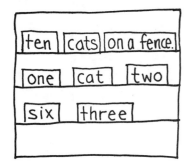

VOCABULARY

All aspects of vocabulary development can be taught in the context of stories the teacher reads to the students. This method models good strategies that the students can later apply to their own reading.

Recognize Word Meanings

Roots/Prefixes

Synonyms/ Antonyms

Unfamiliar Words in Context

COMPREHENSION

Comprehension skills are vital to the reading process. They form the core of all teaching, regardless of subject matter. True comprehension involves analyzing aspects of a text far beyond the simple details of the story. For emergent readers, however, details and other aspects of literal comprehension are necessary stepping stones to more advanced levels of understanding. Inferential concepts and critical thinking skills should be introduced to emergent learners after literal comprehension skills have been mastered. The strategies students develop for literal comprehension skills will continue to be applied as students become more confident readers.

Literal Comprehension

Details

Discussion
Discuss details of story with students.

Draw Picture
Students draw a picture of the story with all details and explain to partner or teacher.

Triarama
Students construct a triarama with story details in it and explain to partner or teacher.

Pronoun Reference

Discussion
Discuss with students who pronouns refer to in story.

Following Directions
Read section of story asking students to draw a picture of who "he," "she," "it," "they," "we" refer to.

Write/Dictate Story
Students write or dictate stories using pronouns.

Sequence

<u>Chain Story Events</u>
Students write and draw the sequence of events in a story.

<u>Flip Books</u>
Students draw and write the beginning and ending of a story. (NOTE: Encourage invented spelling.)

<u>Pocket Chart</u>
Have students arrange words and phrases of predictable books in a pocket chart.

<u>Puppets</u>
Have students act out a story with puppets.

Inferential Comprehension

Relate Story to Personal Experiences

<u>Discussion</u>
Ask children to think of story incidents similar to events in their own lives and discuss them with the class.

<u>Journal</u>
Students draw or write reactions to story characters or events and relate them to personal experiences.

<u>Drawing Similarities</u>
Students draw or write ways they and story characters are similar.

Main Idea

Alexander and the terrible, horrible, no good, very bad day!

The rotten day

How bad can it get?

I think I'll move to Australia.

Ducks can swim

Discussion
Model how to ascertain a main idea by thinking aloud about the story's title and main events.

Brainstorm Other Titles
Students discuss other titles the book or story could have and why.

Shape Books
Students make a shape book and draw or write a story based on the book's shape, then read it to a partner or adult.

Cause / Effect

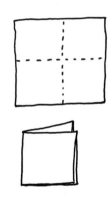

Discussion/Instruction
Ask students to think of cause/effect relationships in their own lives. Then model how to find these relationships in the story by thinking aloud about characters and situations.

Categorize Pictures
Bring to class picture cards, some with pictures of causes and some with effects. Have children categorize or match them.

Fold Books
Students draw or write a story and read it to a friend.

Draw Conclusions

Discussion
Provide plenty of practice for students to draw conclusions from story passages.

Chart Story
Write a chart story about what children think will happen before the story is finished.

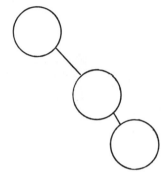

Chaining
Chain what kids think will happen as a result of a character's actions or a situation.

Puppets
Students act out stories with puppets.

Predict Outcomes

Discussion
Allow students numerous opportunities to predict the outcome of the story.

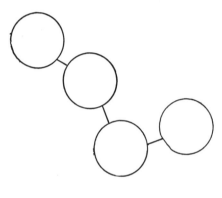

Chain Events
Students write and draw the sequence of events in a story, or the events that might happen in a story.

Puppets
Students act out a story with puppets.

Compare / Contrast

Discussion
Compare and contrast characters and events from the story with those of the children's lives.

Flip Book
Students draw or write how characters or events are the same and different in the story.

Venn Diagram
Students compare and contrast familiar objects.

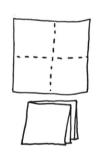

Fold Book
Students draw or write a story and read it to a friend.

Critical Thinking

Analyze Character / Setting / Plot

Discussion
Ask students probing questions about characters, setting, and plot. Relate all of these story elements to the students' personal experiences.

Story Frame
Students draw or write characters, setting, or plot of story. (NOTE: Start with character and setting first.)

Act Out A Character
Students act out the characters in a story.

Real / Make Believe

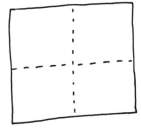

Discussion
Discuss with students the different story elements that are either real or make-believe.

Fold Book
Students write a real or make-believe story.

Act It Out
Students act out real or make-believe elements of a story.

Good study skills are critical. They teach students methods for finding information (a precursor to research) and how to interpret information in the form of maps, charts, and graphs. Students need to develop strategies for finding information as early as possible. Maps, charts, and graphs, as well as book parts, should be introduced to the emergent learner.

Maps / Charts / Graphs

Discussion

Introduce the basic elements found on maps, charts, and graphs, and tell students the types of information each resource provides.

Developing Own Maps/ Charts / Graphs

After learning about maps, charts, and graphs, students construct their own.

Small Group Interpretation

In reading or math groups, ask students how many things they can tell from a map, chart, or graph.

Book Parts

Discussion/Instruction

Introduce book parts each time a new story is begun. Point out front and back covers, title pages, and tables of contents.

Book Covers

Students design covers for favorite books, making sure to include authors' and illustrators' names.

Authoring Books

Students write their own stories and design their own books with title pages.

Developing learners have mastered the basics of reading and writing. Improving those skills is the next step. This is best accomplished by introducing students to whole contexts, with whole stories and concepts providing a base for learning.

Each of the reading and comprehension skills for developing learners listed on the Scope and Sequence Chart of Whole Language Skills (page 51) is analyzed in depth on the following pages (65-74).

TEACHER READS ALOUD DAILY

A mixture of picture books and chapter books are excellent sources for developing learners to hear read aloud. (A list of books recommended for developing learners is provided in chapter 12, pages 140-156.) The teacher should model reading fluency by reading aloud from a variety of books of varying lengths.

Picture Book
Discuss author, title page, illustrator, etc. (work into study skills).

Chapter Books
Ask such questions as "Remember what happened yesterday?"

Read Along
Encourage students to follow along in class books or big books.

STUDENTS READ SILENTLY EVERY DAY

Time should be set aside each day for students to choose their own books and find comfortable places to read silently. The teacher needs to read during this time also in order to model reading as a life skill.

DEVELOPING LEARNERS
Silent Reading
15-25 minutes

STUDENTS READ IN OTHER SITUATIONS DAILY

Developing learners need a variety of reading opportunities which enhance their comprehension skills and fluency. Some options include their participation in guided reading, paired reading, conference reading, various literature activities, a listening post, and independent reading activities.

Guided Reading
(Similar to reading groups.) Meet with small groups for reading skills instruction. Guide students through a literature book.

Paired Reading
Students read to each other in pairs from the same books.

Conference Reading
Meet with students individually to assess comprehension and oral reading skills.

Literature Activities
Read a literature story aloud. (Use books with descriptive language.) After a class discussion, students complete a related activity.

Listening Post
Students listen to a taped story and follow along in their books.

Independent Reading
Students read stories independently and keep track of them in a reading log.

WORD IDENTIFICATION

The developing learner needs to gain a large repertoire of sight words. This goal can be met by providing students with opportunities to participate in the many different reading situations previously outlined. By the time phonics instruction is completed at the end of the second grade, children should understand the alphabet well enough to approach unfamiliar words and decode them fairly well. Developing readers should also be able to use clues in a story's context to estimate the pronunciation of unknown words.

cannot = can't

* take from reading

Billy's words

avoid

<u>Phonics</u>
Teach vowel sounds and "silent e" rule. Complete instruction by the end of second grade.

<u>Contractions/compound words</u>
Give direct instruction for these. Have students apply their knowledge in writing.

<u>Sight Words</u>
Avoid giving word lists and flashcards out of context. Once children master words, let them use them in their stories.

VOCABULARY

Vocabulary development skills should be taught to developing learners by using unfamiliar words from reading assignments. Avoid teaching word lists in isolation; students won't retain knowledge unless they can apply and use it in meaningful ways.

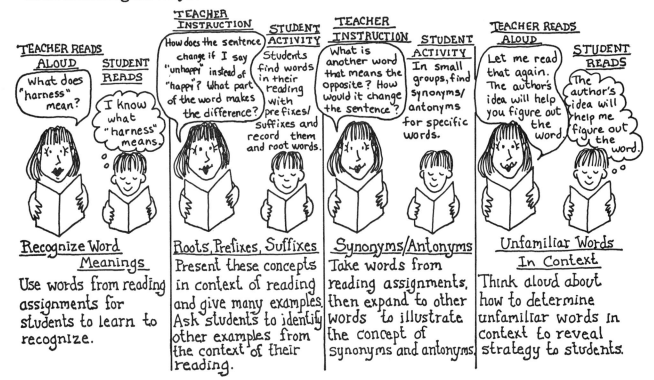

<u>TEACHER READS ALOUD</u>
What does "harness" mean?

<u>STUDENT READS</u>
I know what "harness" means.

<u>TEACHER INSTRUCTION</u>
How does the sentence change if I say "unhappy" instead of "happy"? What part of the word makes the difference?

<u>STUDENT ACTIVITY</u>
Students find words in their reading with prefixes/ suffixes and record them and root words.

<u>TEACHER INSTRUCTION</u>
What is another word that means the opposite? How would it change the sentence?

<u>STUDENT ACTIVITY</u>
In small groups, find synonyms/ antonyms for specific words.

<u>TEACHER READS ALOUD</u>
Let me read that again. The author's idea will help you figure out the word.

<u>STUDENT READS</u>
The author's idea will help me figure out the word.

<u>Recognize Word Meanings</u>
Use words from reading assignments for students to learn to recognize.

<u>Roots, Prefixes, Suffixes</u>
Present these concepts in context of reading and give many examples. Ask students to identify other examples from the context of their reading.

<u>Synonyms/Antonyms</u>
Take words from reading assignments, then expand to other words to illustrate the concept of synonyms and antonyms.

<u>Unfamiliar Words In Context</u>
Think aloud about how to determine unfamiliar words in context to reveal strategy to students.

Developing learners are ready to tackle advanced comprehension skills in the areas of literal comprehension, inferential comprehension, and critical thinking.

Literal Comprehension
It is important for students to acquire a basic understanding of literal comprehension before springboarding into inferential and critical thinking skills.

Details

Discussion
Discuss, as well as point out, story details so that students will understand the process.

Chaining
Chain story details.

Story Frame
Students write story details for the beginning, middle, and ending of story.

Retell/Act Out Story
Students retell or act out the story events. This involves intimate knowledge of story details.

Pronoun Reference

Discussion
Hold an informal discussion about to whom or what "he/she/it/his/hers/theirs" refers.

Rewrite Story
Students rewrite the story using pronouns.

Draw Pictures
Students draw pictures of to whom or what "he/she/it/his/hers/theirs" refers.

Sequence

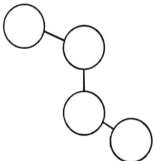

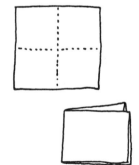

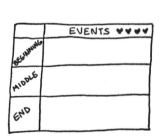

Discussion/Instruction
Discuss and model how to determine sequence of events in story.

Chaining
Students chain story events in proper sequence.

Fold Book
Draw or write major story events in fold book.

Story Map
Students map story events from beginning, middle, and ending of story.

Inferential Comprehension

Acquiring inferential comprehension skills is of foremost importance to developing readers, and discussion and instruction are crucial elements of this process. Students cannot be expected to know how to utilize these skills without first being taught.

Relate Story To Personal Experiences

Discussion
Always help students connect story aspects to their own experiences.

Response Journal
Students write responses to characters and story situations in response journal, also noting personal experiences.

Similarities/Differences
Students draw or write about similarities and differences between their own experiences and those of characters in the story.

Main Idea

Discussion/Instruction
Model how to ascertain main idea by thinking aloud about topic sentences, whole meaning, etc. Practice with paragraphs, then try stories.

Writing Other Titles
Students think of other titles for stories and books and explain why they made their choices.

Story Map
Map out main ideas of paragraphs or sections of a story for students.

Cause/Effect

Discussion/Instruction
Ask students to think of cause and effect relationships in their own lives. Then show them how to find cause and effect relationships in the story by thinking aloud about characters and story events.

Flip Book
Students make a flip book of causes and effects in the story.

Small Group Situation
Skim story passages for cause and effect relationships and discuss.

Draw Conclusions

 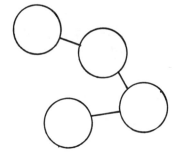 

Discussion
Provide plenty of practice for students to draw conclusions from passages based on story elements and facts.

Chaining
Students chain conclusions drawn about characters or events in story.

Rewrite Ending
Students rewrite a plausible ending to the story.

Predict Outcomes

 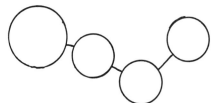  

Discussion
Allow students many opportunities to predict what will happen next in the story.

Chaining
Students chain what might happen if a major aspect of the story were changed.

What Happens Next?
In pairs or small groups, students read sections of a story to others and stop at critical places to ask, "What might happen next?" If the teacher has modeled this behavior often, students will know exactly what to do.

Compare/Contrast

  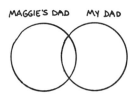  

Discussion/Instruction
Compare and contrast information across the curriculum — in math, science, social studies, etc. This skill comes easily when practiced often.

Flip Book
Students write or draw comparisons between characters, situations, things, etc.

Venn Diagram
Students write or draw similarities and differences between people, places, things, etc.

Small Group Situation
Compare and contrast more detailed information in small groups — setting, author's style, passages, etc

Act Out Story
Two students act out and tell how characters are the same and different.

Critical Thinking

Critical thinking concepts should also be emphasized in the developing learner's curriculum. Small group situations lend themselves to this kind of learning, but there are a variety of ways to structure the discussion and instruction of critical thinking skills.

Analyze Character / Setting

Discussion
Ask probing questions about characters in stories where events are set. Encourage children to get to know characters "like friends."

Story Frame
Students write characters and setting details in a frame that covers beginning, middle, and end of story.

Character Portrayal
Students portray characters in the story and tell about themselves.

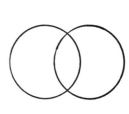

Venn Diagram
Students compare characters or settings.

Small Group Situation
Students write, draw, or discuss other attributes a character might have based on story details.

Real / Make-Believe

Discussion
Make this a part of reading aloud as well as reading group discussions, so students can think about and categorize events.

Fold Book
Students detail either real or make-believe events that happen in the story.

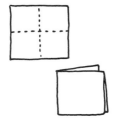

Story Map
Students write or draw real or make-believe events that happen in the story.

Flip Book
Students write or draw and categorize real and make-believe events in the story.

Small Group Situation
Make up either real or make-believe events that could happen in the story based on information about characters and situations.

Summarize Plot

Discussion/Instruction
Guide students step-by-step through writing a summary of story events.

Story Frame
Students summarize story plot.

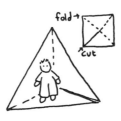

Triarama
Students construct a triarama and write a summary of the story on it.

Narrate Story and Act it Out
Students narrate and act out a story.

Small Group Situation
Students summarize the story as a group.

Study skills will become increasingly important to developing learners; therefore, as early as possible, they need to understand the concepts and methods of research. This can be an enjoyable learning process and should be made fun for the teacher and the students. Once again, discussion and instruction of study skills topics are vital to this learning process. Small groups are a great medium in which to promote successful study skills.

Maps / Charts / Graphs

Discussion / Instruction
Discuss the types of information that can and cannot be learned from reading maps, charts, and graphs.

Developing Own Maps/ Charts/Graphs
Have students construct their own maps, charts, or graphs as class, group, or individual projects in areas of math, science, social studies, and reading.

Plan Trips
Using maps, students can plan and plot imaginary trips, citing destinations and logging miles traveled. Have them keep a diary of each day's adventure.

Books Parts

Discussion/Instruction
Always show or discuss book parts when reading aloud or in small groups.

Title Page/ Table of Contents/ Index
During the course of reading, students cite information shown on various book parts.

Write Own Books
Students write and illustrate their own books, including tables of contents and title pages.

Small Group Situations
Students formulate questions related to a book's index and exchange them with those of another group.

Alphabetization

Discussion/Instruction
Provide many fun and informal alphabetizing activities in order that students not come to view this task as a chore.

Alphabetizing/ Categorizing Cards
This activity is easily paired with card catalog activities. Students alphabetize cards by title, author, or subject.

ABC Books
Students write or draw their own ABC books related to a topic being discussed or a story being read in class.

Alphabetize Spelling Words
This activity can be implemented along with each week's spelling words.

Small Group Situations
Students alphabetize books in a class library by title or author.

Dictionary

Discussion/Instruction
Model the use of the dictionary as a common tool. When reading aloud, frequently use the dictionary to look up unfamiliar words.

Personal Dictionaries
Students maintain personal dictionaries of words they do not know.

Dictionary Experiences
Students look up spelling words, unfamiliar vocabulary words from reading assignments, etc. as a natural part of the learning process.

Small Groups
Small groups of students can race to see who can look up a word the fastest, as well as give information about it and use it correctly in a sentence.

Reference

Discussion/Instruction
Make available menus, magazines, phone books, etc. for student use.

Telephone Book
Play "Whom Do You Call?", a game in which the teacher (or students) cites a problem and then students search in the yellow pages for whom to call.

Newspaper/Class Paper
Reading groups take turns compiling a class newspaper after researching how actual newspapers are put together.

Atlas
Students use the atlas to make their own maps, citing rivers and other geographical formations in their community.

Quick Reports/Encyclopedia
Students summarize information or glean main idea about a topic in an encyclopedia.

Small Groups
Students play "Fast Facts," a game in which groups review all types of references for facts about a particular subject.

Card Catalog

Library Search
1. Three authors of fiction whose last names start with X, Y, or Z.
2. Titles of three poetry books.
3. Two books you would use to research sharks.

<u>Discussion/Instruction</u>
Bring students to the library for real experiences with card catalog. Have students use the card catalog to look up required reading assignments.

<u>Class/Individual Card Catalogs</u>
Maintain a class card catalog of books read aloud. Students can maintain their own cards with correct bibliographic information about each book they have read.

<u>Personal Reading Logs</u>
Card catalog information about each book a student reads can be entered into personal reading logs.

<u>Small Group Situation</u>
Students complete a library search similar to a scavenger hunt. They can look for specific types of books and authors. Students can also design a library search of their own.

It is conceivable that some classrooms will have a mixture of developing and fluent readers. Both can be easily accommodated in the same room since many of their learning experiences are similar. Simply refer to both sections, "Developing Learners" and "Fluent Learners," for strategies and ideas.

FLUENT LEARNERS (Grades 4-6)

Fluent learners need to enhance their inferential and critical thinking skills and master study skills by frequent practice with reference materials. The most pressing need for fluent learners, however, is to develop strategies for the various types of reading they are asked to do. Supplemental reading and comprehension activities for each skills area listed on the Scope and Sequence Chart of Whole Language Skills (page 51) are provided on pages 74-83. These activities reflect the belief that fluent learners are capable of a great deal of independent work.

TEACHER READS ALOUD DAILY

Fluent learners should hear both chapter books and selected picture books read aloud daily by the teacher. A list of books recommended for fluent learners is available in chapter 12 (pages 140-156). Before, during, and after books are read aloud, the teacher should ask probing questions in order that students think carefully about the information being read.

Think about how Bert and Jennie are the same and different in this chapter.
<u>COMPARE/CONTRAST</u>
<u>ANALYZE CHARACTER</u>

<u>MOOD</u>
Listen for how the author describes the setting and how that sets the mood for the story.

Listen for the problem Karana is faced with. What would you do in that situation? What do you think she will do?
<u>DRAWING CONCLUSIONS</u>
<u>PREDICTING OUTCOMES</u>

The teacher should read aloud at least once a day. Twice a day would be preferable.

STUDENTS READ SILENTLY EVERY DAY

Research indicates that upper elementary and middle school children should read silently for approximately two hours a week. In the classroom, this equates to a minimum of 25 minutes per day. It is important for teachers to model reading as a life skill by bringing in their own recreational reading during this time. Silent reading sessions work well after recess or P.E. as they provide a nice contrast to physical activity. Structure the day so that students automatically know when to grab a book and read.

STUDENTS READ IN OTHER SITUATIONS DAILY

A great deal can be accomplished in individual and small group reading situations with fluent readers. Because they have mastered the basics of comprehension, fluent learners can complete preparatory reading activities before coming to the reading group. Guided reading sessions are organized much like traditional reading groups. Activity suggestions for before, during, and after guided reading sessions follow:

Before Guided Reading Activities

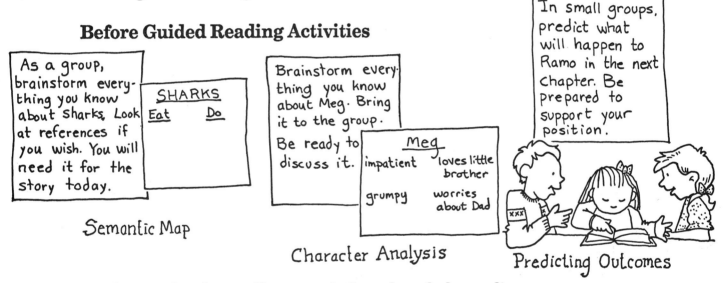

As a group, brainstorm everything you know about sharks. Look at references if you wish. You will need it for the story today.

SHARKS
Eat   Do

Semantic Map

Brainstorm everything you know about Meg. Bring it to the group. Be ready to discuss it.

Meg
impatient   loves little brother
grumpy   worries about Dad

Character Analysis

In small groups, predict what will happen to Ramo in the next chapter. Be prepared to support your position.

Predicting Outcomes

While meeting in small groups before the whole reading group convenes, students can be asked to think critically about certain aspects of the story. In small groups, students are also able to practice working with others, which is a crucial skill.

During Guided Reading Activities

When meeting with fluent learner reading groups, teachers should immediately ask for the students' ideas or work from the Before Guided Reading Activity. Their work should be discussed and students allowed to do most of the talking as it is their thinking processes that are important. Teachers should then guide the students into the reading selection (it is assumed most selections will be taken from literature books with some from other sources, such as basals, magazines, and newspapers).

After Guided Reading Activities

After guided reading, the teacher should discuss the aspect of the story for which the students have read and then issue a seatwork assignment which integrates all of the activities. Doing this involves the students in real learning, reading, and writing experiences that challenge them and force them to think on levels no workbook assignment could duplicate.

Other reading activities include:

Read to Younger Children
Students can visit K-2 classrooms and read aloud to small groups of children.

Record-a-Thought
Students prepare a character portrayal, short story, favorite passage, book talk etc, and record it on tape for others to hear at the listening center.

Independent Reading
Students read books independently and record them in a personal reading log.

Paired Reading
Students in pairs read to each other from the same books.

Listening Center
Students listen to recorded stories that other classmates have made.

Scrapbook
Students cut and paste magazine and newspaper articles into a scrapbook and record reactions.

VOCABULARY

Note that Word Identification is absent from the scope and sequence chart of fluent readers' skills (page 51). This is because students do not need to dwell on how to approach unfamiliar words as it is assumed they have already acquired the skills to do that. Fluent learners do need to broaden their vocabulary development skills; however, care should be taken not to present lists of vocabulary words that are unrelated to anything else in the students' studies. All vocabulary words should come from student reading assignments.

Recognize Word Meanings
List words and their meanings on the board and discuss them so that students can better understand their reading assignments.

Roots, Prefixes, Suffixes
Discuss meaning of prefixes and suffixes and their root words. Have students skim passages for examples.

Synonyms/Antonyms
Use words from reading assignments and discuss synonyms and antonyms. Have students read or write passages substituting synonyms and antonyms; discuss how the meaning of the sentence changes.

Unfamiliar Words in Context
Help students by reasoning aloud how to derive the meaning of an unfamiliar word; students can practice the strategy on their own.

COMPREHENSION

Fluent learners need to spend the majority of their time developing strategies to enhance both their inferential comprehension and critical thinking skills.

Literal Comprehension
Literal comprehension skills should be introduced only as a springboard to more advanced levels of comprehension.

Details / Pronoun Reference / Sequence

Discussion
Discuss story details and their sequence. (Pronoun reference naturally becomes a part of this process.) Use this information to springboard into inferential and critical comprehension skills.

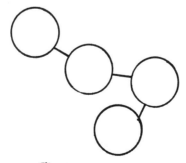

Chaining
Sequence story events in a story chain.

Story Frame
Recount story details in a story frame.

DETAILS

Beginning

Middle

End

Inferential Comprehension

Fluent learners should concentrate on increasing their inferential comprehension and critical thinking skills. The following activities can be used as individual exercises or as Before Guided Reading activities. Small group situations are ideal for teaching these skills.

Relate Story to Experience

Discussion / Instruction
To heighten comprehension, always prompt students to think or discuss their own experiences in relation to the story.

Compare/Contrast
Students compare and contrast character traits and story situations with their own experiences.

Response Journal
Students write about personal experiences and reactions to the text being read.

Parallel Story With Own Life
Students are asked to parallel story events with on-going personal events.

Main Idea

Discussion/Instruction
Review paragraphs one at a time to illustrate the author's main idea. Point out that topic sentences usually appear at the beginning or ending of a paragraph.

Paragraph/ Passage Dissection
Students read specific paragraphs for topic sentences. They can jot down significant information that points to a main idea.

Other Titles
Students choose alternate titles for chapters and books and explain why they made their choices.

Skim for Overall Picture
Students skim paragraphs and passages for specific ideas and topic sentences that reveal the main idea.

Cause / Effect

 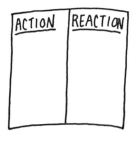  

Discussion/Instruction
Relate reading assignments to students' own lives. Guide them to read for specific cause/ effect relationships.

Action/Reaction
Students list character actions and subsequent reactions in a book's chapter or the entire story. 78

Character Development
Students map the development of each character in a story, showing the various changes each character undergoes.

Small Group Situation
Students brainstorm general cause/effect relationships or those found in a particular story.

Draw Conclusions

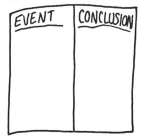

Discussion/Instruction
Encourage students to cite story events and draw conclusions from them. Model this behavior when reading aloud.

Map Events
Students map story events and draw conclusions from them.

Critique Author's Ending
Ask students to decide whether or not they feel the author's ending is good. Have them rewrite the ending based on story events.

Small Group Situation
List each significant story event and brainstorm to come up with what could have happened next as a result.

Predict Outcomes

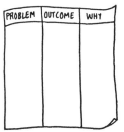

Discussion/Instruction
Create a safe atmosphere in which students can feel comfortable predicting story outcomes. Model how to consider previous story events when predicting outcomes.

Problem / Likely Outcome
Students write down story or chapter problems, their likely outcomes, and the reasons for their decisions.

Chain Ideas
Students predict story outcomes using a chain format. Students can also change a major story event and chain its outcome.

Small Group Situation
Students map outcomes of story events and predict possible character reactions, setting changes, etc.

Compare/Contrast

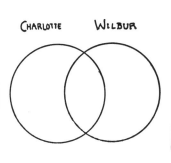

Discussion/Instruction
Provide students with many opportunities to compare and contrast information in the areas of math, science, social studies, etc.

Venn Diagram
Students compare and contrast story characters, situations, etc. using the Venn diagram.

Character Dialog
Students invent character dialog to illustrate the ways in which particular characters are similar or different.

Small Group Situation
Students compare and contrast complex issues, such as authors style, setting, entire themes of particular books, two newspaper articles, two drawings, etc.

Critical Thinking

Critical thinking is an area of learning that has few, if any, right or wrong answers. It deals not in absolutes, but in impressions, tone, and the assessment of how and why an author wrote a particular work. The importance of this area of learning cannot be stressed enough.

Analyze Character / Setting

Discussion/ Instruction
Think aloud about setting and characters' personalities and motives as you read to the students.

Story Frame
Students complete a story frame of characters, setting, and plot for the beginning, middle, and ending of story.

Character Portrayal
Students dress up as characters in the story and explain what happens to them.

Character Caddy
Students draw, write, and collect items the characters might have in their purses or pockets. Have them explain each of their choices using evidence from the story.

Small Group Situation
Students discuss other aspects of character and setting.

Summarize Plot

Discussion/ Instruction
As you begin to read aloud each day, summarize the story up to the point at which you stopped. Ask students to provide input.

Rewrite As A Picture Book
Students rewrite the story as a young child's picture book.

Story Frame
Students complete story frame summarizing the plot for the beginning, middle, and ending of the story.

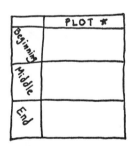

Narrate Story Pantomine
Have one student narrate the story as another acts it out.

Small Group Situation
Students read chapters from the story and summarize it from one character's point of view

Fact/Opinion

Discussion/Instruction
As books are being read aloud, discuss with students whether various elements are fact or opinion and why.

Advertisements
Students create advertisements for books making use of their knowledge of fact and opinion.

Flip Book
Students make a flip book listing story facts and opinions.

Small Group Situation
Students debate opinions and establish positions on a variety of issues.

Mood

Discussion/Instruction
Think aloud about the mood of a particular passage. Point out specific words and phrases which help to set the mood of the story.

Poster of Scene
Students draw pictures of particular scenes and describe them using vivid words and phrases.

Rewrite Figurative Language
Students rewrite certain passages which set the story's mood.

Small Group Situation
Students choose words or phrases from particular passages which illustrate a story's mood. The group then presents their findings to the entire class.

Author's Tone/Intent

Discussion/Instruction
Read aloud to students often so they will become accustomed to hearing and understanding the subtleties of tone and intent.

Key Phrases
Students pick out key phrases that illustrate a book's tone.

Author Portrayal
Have students explain from the author's point of view why the book was written.

Small Group Situation
Groups study a particular passage, examining it for the author's tone and intent. They can also present findings to class.

STUDY SKILLS

Fluent readers should have extensive practice with all areas of study skills. These activities are quite effective when conducted in small group situations.

Maps/Charts/Graphs

Discussion/Instruction
Continually use maps, charts, and graphs to illustrate concepts in the areas of math, science, and social studies.

Design Own Maps/Charts/Graphs
Students design their own maps, charts, and graphs.

Research/Analyze
Have students find charts, graphs, and maps in magazines and newspapers. They can then analyze the types of information each source provides.

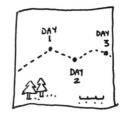

Plan Trips
Students use maps to plan imaginary trips. Have them keep diaries which tell how many miles they travelled each day.

Small Group Situations
Students design a chart or graph which represents some aspect of their group, such as hair length, food eaten, favorite pasttimes, etc

Book Parts

Discussion/Instruction
Always point out a book's title page, index, and table of contents when reading aloud.

Title Page/Index/Table of Contents
Have students write title pages and invent a tables of contents and index pages for various young children's picture books.

Author Own Book
Students write title pages, table of contents, and indexes to accompany stories and reports they write themselves.

Small Group Situation
Students write questions about a book using its index as a source. They can then exchange their questions with those of another group.

Dictionary

Discussion/Instruction
Provide many opportunities for students to work with dictionaries. Consistently use a dictionary when reading aloud to students.

Dictionary vs. Encyclopedia
Students research information in both the dictionary and the encyclopedia.

Personal Dictionary
Students keep personal dictionaries of unfamiliar words from their reading assignments.

Small Group Situation
Groups compile their own dictionaries, or look up spelling and vocabulary words and share with their group.

References

Discussion/Instruction
Provide real experiences for students to work with reference material.

Research One of Each
Students examine different sources for information on a particular topic and record their findings in journals.

Class Atlas
Students compile a class atlas composed of maps of individual desks, the coat closet, activity areas, etc.

Newspaper/Class Paper
Reading groups take turns arranging a class newspaper, or they may compile a newspaper based on the thematic unit currently being studied.

Small Group Situation
Groups research a topic using 3 or 4 different resources, or groups may examine one reference tool and tell what types of information it provides.

Card Catalog

Discussion/Instruction
Instruct students in the use of the card catalog, and then guide them through the process of finding the books they want.

Class Card Catalog
Establish a class card catalog. Each entry should be made by a student who has read the book. The card catalog should be stored in the class library.

Library Search
Hold a fun scavenger hunt for locating books, book titles, authors' names, subjects, etc. in the library's card catalog.

Personal Reading Log
Students keep records of the books they read, listing all information found in the card catalog, including the summary.

Small Group Situation
Groups compile their own library searches using the card catalog.

Chapter Eight

WRITING

The best way to teach children how to write is to give them many opportunities to listen to and read good literature, and then offer just as many opportunities to talk and write about it. Writing well does not merely entail correct spelling, grammar, and punctuation; it also means expressing written ideas on paper the best way children know how. For emergent learners, writing well might mean scribbling a line or two, or writing only the letters heard in each word. Developing learners can express their thoughts more completely, spelling whole words and writing entire sentences. Fluent learners spell most words correctly, and they are able to form sentences into complete stories and paragraphs.

As the writing section of the Scope and Sequence Chart of Whole Language Skills illustrates, writing activities are introduced daily. Both informal and formal experiences should be offered to students at their appropriate learning levels. When students express their thoughts in informal writing activities, spelling and punctuation are not important. These elements do become significant when producing formal writing intended to be read by an audience.

WRITING — Grades	K	1	2	3	4	5	6
Students Write Every Day							
journal/informal/formal writing experiences	x	x	x	x	x	x	x
Spelling							
• invented	x	x	x	x			
• formal		x	x	x	x	x	x
Sentences/Paragraphs							
• teacher writes dictated sentences	x	x	x				
• students complete sentence/story frames	x	x	x				
• write original sentences/paragraphs		x	x	x	x	x	x
• use vivid words (adjectives/adverbs/verbs)		x	x	x	x	x	x
• capitalization/punctuation/grammar		x	x	x	x	x	x
• letter form (personal/business)		x	x	x	x	x	x
• poetry		x	x	x	x	x	x
• organize information for paragraphs/reports			x	x	x	x	x

Spelling is an important skill that students at all grade levels need to learn, but correct spelling should not hinder personal expression. Research into the ways in which children learn reveals that elementary and middle school children can understand more information than they can express. If their written expression is further hindered by the need to spell every word correctly, they will produce far less than they are capable. On the other hand, if spelling is viewed as a skill "under construction," then perfection will not be expected. It is important to remember that spelling is a skill that is being learned and developed by students along with every other whole language skill.

According to recent research, spelling is unrelated to any other reading or writing skill. Here is what we know about it:

1. Spelling is not necessarily related to reading ability. Good readers aren't necessarily good spellers. However, good spellers are always good readers, and poor readers are never good spellers.

2. Spelling is a spatial-relationship skill. Good spellers tend to be right-brained and see words as whole entities rather than as a series of letters

Given these insights into spelling, it would seem that the best way to create good spellers is to expose students to a great deal of printed material and provide them with many opportunities to write.

The term "invented spelling" signifies the type of spelling emergent and developing learners use when approaching a word they do not know. They will write all of the letters they hear in the word and leave out the ones they do not hear. By encouraging children to use invented spelling, the teacher can evaluate the level students have attained in word attack skills. For example, leaving out middle sounds reveals that the child does not hear them; therefore, the teacher knows to stress more medial sounds when teaching.

The instruction emergent learners receive in formal spelling should parallel the phonics instruction they receive (specific activities are outlined in the section of this chapter on emergent learners, pages 86-91). The teaching of formal spelling should continue throughout all grades and learning levels, using as a teaching tool either a formal spelling program, high frequency words, or words from the literature being read in the classroom.

──────┤ **EMERGENT LEARNERS (Grades K-1)** ├──────

Emergent learners need daily writing experiences as much as those students who have already mastered more sophisticated writing skills. The goal for these young learners is to come to view writing as a life skill. The only way to do this is to have students write every day.

STUDENTS WRITE EVERY DAY (Informal/Formal Experiences)

The bulk of emergent learners' writing activities should be informal exercises. The informal writing process stresses oral language: the teacher and the students copy down words, phrases, and sentences spoken in the classroom. This models the connection between oral and written language and serves to familiarize students with the writing process as well.

Oral Language

Dictate Sentences
Children individually dictate sentences to an adult who writes them down. They read them together pointing to each word.

Chart Stories
Teacher writes chart stories dictated by the children. They read together pointing to each word.

Asking Questions
Children ask questions they have pertaining to a field trip or guest speaker. Teacher records them, then reads them pointing to each word.

Writing Experiences

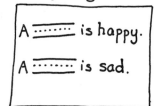

Journals
Children respond to a story or relate personal experiences in their journals. Spelling/punctuation do not matter in journals

Picture Descriptions
Children do their best to write about a picture they have drawn.

Complete Sentence Frame
After brainstorming many ideas the teacher writes on the board, children complete a duplicated sentence frame or copy/complete it from the board.

Formal writing activities are intended for someone outside of the classroom to read. Students should concentrate on their best penmanship, grammar, and spelling skills for this type of writing.

Invitations
Children copy a model written on the board in their best handwriting.

Pen Pals
Pen pals needn't be out of state; they can be in your own district or school. Children exchange letters with another K-1 class or an older 4-6 class for cross-age experiences (answering letters to Santa, Easter Bunny, etc.).

"Published" Books/Stories
Children may want books or stories to be typed and placed in the class library. Correct spelling should be used in these published works.

Most writing exercises should relate somehow to the literature being read by the teacher to the students, and all writing should relate to the thematic unit being studied at the time.

Spelling is a skill that must be learned for writing, just as phonics must be learned for reading. Spelling alone, however, should not drive the writing program just as phonics does not drive the reading program. Young students need to feel comfortable with their emerging writing skills and, therefore, should be encouraged to use invented spelling—the process by which children write words as best they can using whatever decoding skills they have at their disposal. An analysis of invented spelling also reveals the direction further instruction should take.

b c f d w m c g h k l m z	i w t s "I went to the store"	i wt to the str. "I went to the store."	i wint to the store with my mom and we got a big terky to ete frum the frezr sekshun.
Scribbling or strings of random letters	writes initial sounds of words	writes the sounds heard in the words	writes all sounds heard in the words

Scribbling or strings of random letters
DIAGNOSIS: No concept of words or how they are spaced.
PRESCRIPTION: Child helps teacher point to words on next chart story or big book.

writes initial sounds of words
DIAGNOSIS: Good knowledge of beginning and ending sounds.
PRESCRIPTION: Teacher stresses medial vowel sounds in reading group activities.

writes all sounds heard in the words
DIAGNOSIS: Good knowledge of consonants and vowels.
PRESCRIPTION: Ask child if you can write "dictionary spelling" on the largest words. Otherwise, leave the child's spelling alone. It is on the right track.

The more comfortable children feel using invented spelling, they longer their stories will become and the more they will enjoy writing. The more phonics they internalize, the more their spelling will improve, as well. Formal spelling instruction for emergent learners should be consistent with the phonics lessons they are learning in reading. Lessons should begin with the students identifying sounds at the beginning and ending of words. Once children have mastered that skill, instruction can progress to medial vowels. Instruction should cover only one sound at a time, be taught in short sessions of no more than ten or fifteen minutes, and cover no more than eight or ten words at a time.

In box #4, write where you hear the "mmm" sound in the word:
— MAN —
Write if it is at the beginning or end of the word.

An excellent spelling program that uses this approach is *Spelling through Phonics* (Peguis, 1990) by Robert and Marlene McCracken.

SENTENCES/PARAGRAPHS

Emergent learners' writing activities should be based on the literature books and thematic units being studied, then related to the students' personal experiences. In most cases when writing under these circumstances, children will have more to say and will be more likely to view writing as a life skill.

Teacher Writes Dictated Sentences

The beginning of a good developmental writing program involves the teacher writing words and sentences which the students dictate. This process can take several forms:

Describing Pictures
Teacher writes the childrens explanations of their drawings or the retelling of a favorite story or original tale.

BAKERY QUESTIONS
1. Do you make donuts?
2. Do you eat

Chart Stories/Questions
Teacher writes stories or questions the children dictate on chart paper.

The girl is _____.
happy   sad

Pocket Charts
Teacher writes sentence frames on sentence strips. Children dictate words that fit in sentences. Teacher writes them on cards.

After plenty of these activities and teacher prompting, children will begin to try their own hands at writing.

Students Complete Sentence Frame

The second developmental step in the writing process involves the teacher generating discussion based on a book or thematic concept, then writing a sentence frame (an incomplete sentence) on the board. Students brainstorm ideas to complete the sentence frames. After this process, the students either write on a duplicated sentence frame, or copy the sentence frame from the board and complete it. Afterwards, they can draw pictures to illustrate their writing.

FIRST STEP
for those not able to copy from board.

A ____ runs.
cat
dog

Discussion/Brainstorm
Teacher writes sentence frame and brainstorms ideas on board, constantly reading entire sentence frame with each brainstormed word in it.

Fill in Sentence Frame
Children fill in duplicated sentence frame.

FIRST STEP
for those able to copy from board.

A ____ is running and jumping

Discussion/Brainstorm
Teacher writes sentence frame, then writes brainstormed ideas on board.

Copy/Complete Sentence Frame
Children copy and complete sentence frame from board.

Write Original Sentences

After many experiences working with sentence frames, students will naturally begin writing their own sentences if encouraged to do so. Their first attempts may be nothing more than a string of letters, but that is an important step in the writing process.

The cluds are in the sky. ths cld a wzestm

Attempts to copy, then writes strings of letters.

A CAT jumps.
A dg jumps.
A fs jumps.

Fills in sentence frame duplicated on paper. Adds own ideas.

An alligator eats fish. It has sarp tet.

Copies sentence frame from board and extends writing.

Once students have heard numerous stories and participated in chart stories and other group writing experiences, they will innately understand how sentences are combined. The teacher's job, then, is to encourage students to write two sentences by asking them for two ideas about a story or thematic concept.

Tell me what we've learned about bears.

BEARS
Bears are big and furry. They eat fish and berries. They hibernate in the winter.

Instruction
Teacher asks for many ideas about a subject and asks children to copy two of them.

Children Write Two Sentences
Children copy or write two things about the subject.

Use Vivid Words (adjectives/adverbs/verbs)

Instruction is an important aspect of learning how to employ vivid words in writing. The teacher can highlight for students the vivid words in stories read aloud and encourage their use in the students' own writing.

Instruction
Write basic sentence on board or in pocket chart. Have children give ideas for extending it by asking questions: "What kind of dog? What kind of teeth?"

Pocket Chart
Add descriptive words to sentence. Children can manipulate cards on their own.

Chart Story
Ask children to use descriptive words when writing a chart story.

Child's Writing
After all of the experiences, remind children to use vivid words in their stories.

Capitalization/Punctuation/Grammar

Capitalization, punctuation, and grammar are other skills that must be taught, but they are best approached by the teacher in increments. Students should practice only one aspect of capitalization, punctuation, or grammar at a time.

These skills are appropriate for emergent writers:

Capitalization	– "I"
	– Beginning of sentence
Punctuation	– Period at end of sentence
	– Question mark
Grammar	– I/me
	am/are

Instruction
Explain and give many examples of using "I" when referring to self. Write examples children give.

Child's Writing
Children apply "I" when writing a story.

Teacher Correction
Teacher listens to children read their writing, but only corrects for "I" by putting a dot under mistakes so children can correct them.

Child Corrects Writing
Children erase and correct writing mistakes of "I".

90

Letter Form (Personal)

Emergent learners need to learn correct letter form for personal letters only. Again, the teacher instructs and models the format, and the students either complete a duplicated letter frame or copy one from the board.

Instruction
Teacher explains letter form, writes a class-dictated letter, and reads it with them until they can read it themselves.

Complete Duplicated Letter Frame
Young children complete the opening and closing of the letter, but read only the body of it to a partner or teacher.

Copy from Board
Children copy letter from the board and read to teacher or a partner.

Poetry

There should be many opportunities for the teacher to read aloud poetry to the class. Young children enjoy poetry and love chanting and enacting finger plays along with it. Favorite poems can be put on charts which the class reads aloud together.

DEVELOPING LEARNERS (Grades 2-3)

Developing learners need a variety of writing experiences in order to develop the basic skills they have already mastered into more comprehensive forms of communication.

STUDENTS WRITE EVERY DAY

A number of different writing activities can be employed for developing learners. Whatever activities are chosen should correspond to either a literature book being read or the thematic unit being studied. Journal writing should be a daily activity. The journal is primarily an outlet in which students can respond to a book the teacher is reading aloud or a concept currently being studied. Many inferential comprehension and critical thinking concepts are reinforced through this type of writing. A journal can be a composition booklet, a monthly folder with pages stapled together, or single sheets which the students compile into a weekly folder.

Composition Book

Stapled Folder

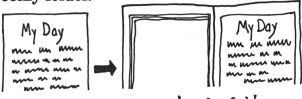

Single sheets compiled into folder

The most effective journal assignments draw on students' personal experiences, and students should brainstorm journal ideas in a group before writing begins. Students should be bursting with ideas when they sit down to write! When students have something to say, they become excited about communicating their ideas. If students have nothing to say, on the other hand, writing becomes an act of drudgery.

For All Journal Assignments

Teacher reads aloud to children using good lesson design.

Discuss or brainstorm ideas with class.

Journal assignments springboard off of discussion/brainstorming.

Sample Journal Assignments

Write and draw a physical description of a character.

(Include behavior and other character traits.)

Describe a Character

Write about an experience you had that was similar to the character's.

Similar Experience

Chain events in the story as though a major element were different.

(example: Little Red Riding Hood and her Grandmother live at the beach)

Chain Events

Write what happens after the end of the story (or chapter) and why.

What Happens Next?

Write what other title you would give to the book/chapter and why.

Another Title

Write a different way the story could have ended and why.

Different Ending

Write/draw how you and the character are the same/different.
-or-
Write how two characters are the same/different.

Same/Different

Write a letter to a character explaining how you feel about what happened in the story.

Write a Letter

What words were used to describe characters, setting, or events in the story? Use them in your own writing.

Describing Words

Give a Gift

Categorizing

Favorite Part

When reading student journal entries, the teacher should respond only to the ideas written. Spelling or punctuation errors should not be corrected.

The informal writing process includes brainstorming ideas and writing rough drafts. These exercises are meant only for the student, group, or teacher to see and do not need to be in sentence form or contain correct spelling or punctuation. Many of the activities for journal writing apply to informal writing exercises; the only difference is that informal writing activities need not be in response to a book. Small group situations are perfect for conducting informal writing experiences.

Informal Writing Assignments

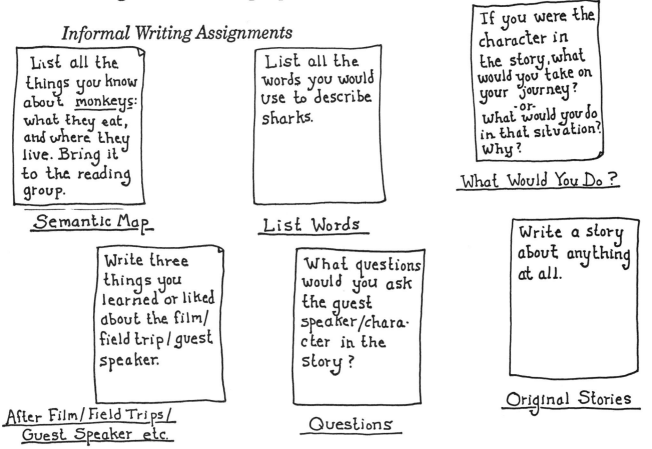

Semantic Map

List Words

What Would You Do ?

After Film / Field Trips /
Guest Speaker etc.

Questions

Original Stories

Time should also be allowed for students to write and illustrate stories on any topic they choose.

Formal writing is intended for an audience to read; therefore, correct spelling, grammar, and punctuation become important. When completing most formal writing exercises, students should follow these processes:

1. Prewriting
2. First Draft
3. Revising
4. Editing
5. Publishing

1. *Prewriting:* Gathering ideas and organizing them.

2. *First Draft:* Writing ideas on paper without regard to spelling, punctuation, grammar, etc.

3. *Revising:* Reread the story or have a partner read it, and listen for areas that need work (more detail, less repetition, clearer language, etc.). Make necessary changes.

4. *Editing:* Check and double-check spelling, punctuation, grammar, etc. Work with a partner to double-check entire work for any last mistakes.

5. *Publishing:* Share it with an audience by completing one or more of these projects:
   • Print or type the story
   • Design a book
   • Read story to class and/or school principal
   • Place in the class library
   • Record story for listening center

All of the formal writing processes are important for students to learn. However, each step should not be made a requirement for everything students write, or their creativity and enthusiasm for writing could be dampened.

SPELLING

Invented spelling is acceptable for larger words that developing learners do not know how to spell correctly; however, students at this level should spell familiar and high-frequency words correctly, or at least include all of a word's consonants and most of its vowels. When reading students' papers, ask them if you may write the "dictionary spelling" of larger words beneath their invented spelling. If they agree (which they usually do), write the correct spelling underneath the word. Students can then copy this word into notebooks containing their personal dictionaries.

Student Writing
Most familiar words are spelled correctly because daily reading and writing assignments provide constant practice.

Teacher Corrects
Teacher asks to write "dictionary spelling" underneath familiar words.

Personal Dictionary
Students write unfamiliar words in their personal dictionaries.

Instruction in formal spelling should continue with an emphasis on phonetics until the end of second grade. By then, all major phonetics' rules will have been practiced and learned. It is important to remember not to teach these rules in isolation, but to apply them to student reading assignments.

Spelling is consistent with phonetic principles taught and applied by end of second grade.

Spelling words from thematic units or literature books.

Selectively use formal spelling programs.

After the second grade, formal spelling instruction should emphasize words learned in thematic units or encountered in literature. If a commercial spelling program is used, selectively choose words and activities from it, too.

SENTENCES/PARAGRAPHS

Complete Story Frames
Story frames are also known as story starters. Use literature or thematic units to determine story starters, and always preface writing exercises with discussion or brainstorming sessions to develop student ideas. The story starters should also be related to the thematic unit being taught to allow students to incorporate and apply the information they have already learned.

Write Original Sentences/Paragraphs

Encourage developing writers to extend their writing to tell complete stories by giving them ample time to write and relaxing spelling and punctuation concerns. Students should be able to share their stories immediately, either with a partner, parent helper, teacher's aide, or the teacher. This also encourages writing.

Instruction must be given if students are to understand the concept of paragraphs. While reading aloud or in reading groups, the teacher should point out paragraphs and ask students to read paragraphs for specific information. Only after they understand the concept of paragraphing should they be asked to write paragraphs of their own.

Original Stories (Sentences)

Allow Ample Time
Give children ample time to write and develop stories.

Relax Spelling and Punctuation Concerns
Informal writing is important for its length and fluency. Spelling and punctuation shouldn't matter.

Immediate Feedback
Students are able to immediately read their stories to someone else.

Paragraphs

Point Out Paragraphs
Teacher points out paragraphs when reading aloud. Instructs students on paragraph indentation.

Students Read Paragraphs
Students read paragraphs in reading group. Teacher leads guided reading.

Write Paragraphs
After discussing indenting and ideas for paragraphs, students write their own.

Use Vivid Words (Adjectives/Adverbs/Verbs)

From the reading the students are doing, the teacher can extract sentences and paragraphs with vivid words and begin instruction on this concept. After students understand the concept of vivid words, they should immediately apply their knowledge by writing their own stories using vivid words. Journal assignments are perfect outlets in which to apply this skill.

Vivid Passage Read
Teacher directs students to listen or read for vivid words in description.

Instruction
Teacher writes words on board that students dictate. They discuss why vivid words are powerful.

Journal Assignments
Teacher gives journal assignment for students to use vivid words.

Capitalization/Punctuation/Grammar

Correct capitalization, punctuation, and grammar skills become more important as students' writing develops; therefore, time should be set aside for instruction and practice in these areas.

Appropriate skills for developing writers are:

Capitalization	– Beginning of sentence – "I" – Proper Nouns
Punctuation	– . ? ! – Commas in a series
Grammar	– subject/verb agreement – I/me – too/to/two

Students should have ample opportunities to apply these skills in real situations, not merely on workbook pages. When practicing a particular skill the teacher should correct for that skill alone.

I had milk, orange juice, and toast for breakfast. I had cereal, too. COMMAS

Teacher Corrects for Skill
The teacher only reads and corrects for the specific skill being taught.

Child Corrects Paper
Children correct their mistakes to apply new knowledge.

97

Letter Form (Personal)

The personal letter is the only letter format developing learners need to know. Pen pals, thank-you letters, and notes home to parents are good letter-writing experiences for the developing learner.

Pen Pals: Write letters to students in other countries, states, schools in district, classes at same school.

Story Characters: Write letters to characters from a book or story.

Thank-You Letters: Write thank-you letters to guest speakers and for field trips, special events, etc.

Notes Home: Write letters inviting parents to special class functions.

Poetry

Writing poetry can be a powerful tool for teaching vivid words, as well as for reinforcing concepts learned during a thematic unit. Rhyming poems are enjoyable, but other forms of poetry can be introduced to developing learners.

Cinquain (4-line version)

Pig   (one noun)
smooth, curly-tailed   (two adjectives)
wiggling, squealing, trotting   (three verbs)
Piggie-pork   (synonym)

Picture Poetry

getting mail and reading it. Valentine's day is my favorite day. It makes me feel special. I like

Organize Information for Paragraphs

Learning how to organize information into paragraph format is important to developing learners because it is a skill necessary for writing reports. The best tool with which to teach organizational skills is the semantic map. Once students complete a semantic map, they can write a sentence for each section of the map and then form their sentences into paragraphs.

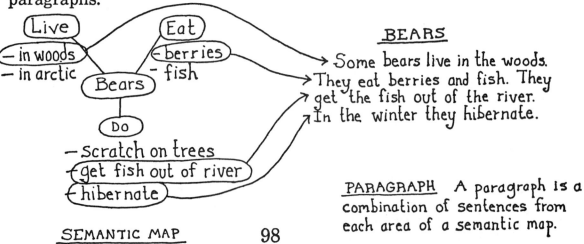

Live
— in woods
— in arctic

Eat
— berries
— fish

Bears

Do
— scratch on trees
— get fish out of river
— hibernate

BEARS

Some bears live in the woods. They eat berries and fish. They get the fish out of the river. In the winter they hibernate.

PARAGRAPH A paragraph is a combination of sentences from each area of a semantic map.

SEMANTIC MAP   98

Fluent learners need practice with a variety of writing formats to develop a fluency and ease in writing for different audiences, organizing ideas into report form, and applying writing as a life skill.

STUDENTS WRITE EVERY DAY

Fluent learners' writing activities should flow naturally from the literature books read and thematic units studied. Just as there is time scheduled every day for silent reading, it is a good idea to set aside 15-20 minutes of silent writing time each day, as well. These exercises can be completed in the students' journals or written using any other format they wish.

Journals

Journal writing should be a daily activity in which students respond to either the book the teacher is reading aloud or books the students are reading silently. Journals are an excellent way for students to practice their critical thinking and inferential comprehension skills.

Discussion/Brainstorming
As with all the writing assignments, discussion and brainstorming are necessary to stimulate student ideas.

Journal Assignment
Journal assignment springs naturally from brainstorming done prior to writing.

Sample Journal Assignments

If you were in the character's situation, what would you do? why?

Analyze Character Situation

Write a letter from one character to another, explaining his or her point of view.

Point of View Letter

Make up a new title for the chapter and explain why you chose it.

New Chapter Title

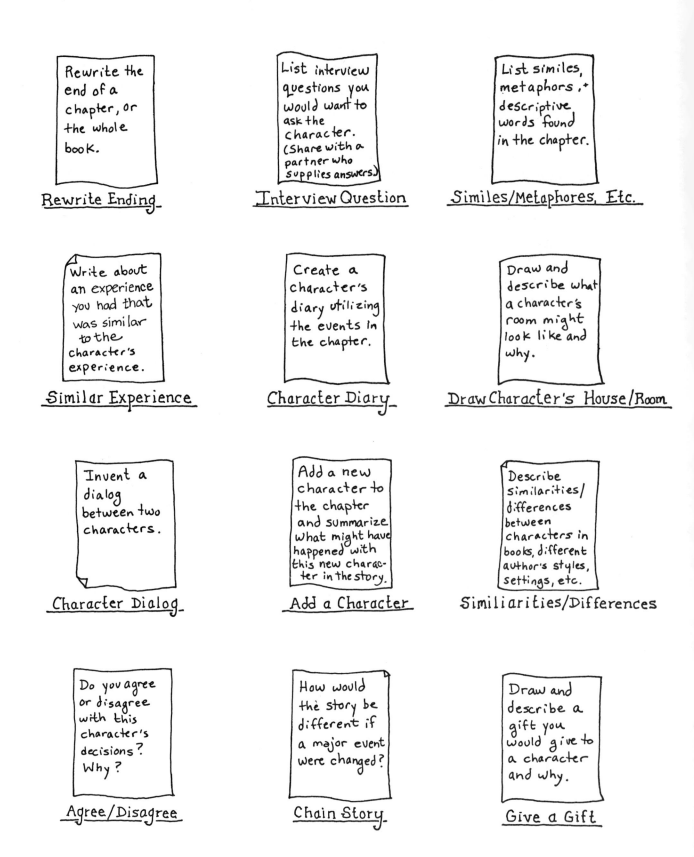

Rewrite Ending

Rewrite the end of a chapter, or the whole book.

Interview Question

List interview questions you would want to ask the character. (Share with a partner who supplies answers.)

Similes/Metaphores, Etc.

List similes, metaphors, + descriptive words found in the chapter.

Similar Experience

Write about an experience you had that was similar to the character's experience.

Character Diary

Create a character's diary utilizing the events in the chapter.

Draw Character's House/Room

Draw and describe what a character's room might look like and why.

Character Dialog

Invent a dialog between two characters.

Add a Character

Add a new character to the chapter and summarize what might have happened with this new character in the story.

Similiarities/Differences

Describe similarities/ differences between characters in books, different author's styles, settings, etc.

Agree/Disagree

Do you agree or disagree with this character's decisions? Why?

Chain Story

How would the story be different if a major event were changed?

Give a Gift

Draw and describe a gift you would give to a character and why.

Teachers should respond only to student ideas when reading journal entries. Spelling and punctuation do not matter in this format; only thinking processes and ideas are important.

Informal Writing

Informal writing assignments are not intended for an audience and are perfect activities for reading groups to complete before meeting with the teacher.

Informal Writing Assignments:

Brainstorm ways a character can solve his or her problem, how the chapter should end, etc.

Brainstorming

Map everything you know about a subject, then list where you might find other information.

Semantic Map

Formulate questions you want answered in the next chapter.

Questions

List what you would take on a character's journey.

What Would You Do?

List words describing the character up to a particular point in the book.

Describe Character

Chain the plot of the story, or what might happen if a major event in the story were changed.

Chaining

Describe a character's thoughts and feelings throughout a chapter's events.

Point of View

Write an original story about anything you want.

Original Story

List or draw three things you learned or liked about the film, speaker, or fieldtrip.

After Film/Speaker/Fieldtrip

Allow plenty of time for informal writing as it reinforces the concept of writing as a life skill.

Formal Writing

Because formal writing is intended to be read by an audience, elements such as spelling, punctuation, and grammar are important. Students should apply these processes to most formal writing assignments:

> 1. Prewriting
> 2. First Draft
> 3. Revising
> 4. Editing
> 5. Publishing

1. *Prewriting:* Gathering ideas and organizing them.

2. *First Draft:* Writing ideas on paper without regard to spelling, punctuation, grammar, etc.

3. *Revising:* Reread the story or have a partner read it back, and listen for places that need work (more detail, less repetition, clearer language, etc.). Make necessary changes.

4. *Editing:* Check and double-check spelling, punctuation, grammar, etc. Work with a partner to double-check the entire work for any last mistakes.

5. *Publishing:* Share it with an audience by completing one or more of these projects:
   - Print or type the story.
   - Design a book.
   - Read story to class and/or school principal.
   - Place in class library.
   - Record story for listening center.

Type story

Make book

Place in class library

Record story

Invented spelling is acceptable for fluent learners in journal or informal writing assignments only. Even in these media, invented spelling should be the exception and not the rule. For the most part, fluent learners should employ formal spelling rules in their work.

Spelling words for fluent learners should be pulled from thematic units being studied or the literature books being read. If a commercial spelling program is required, selectively choose words and activities from it.

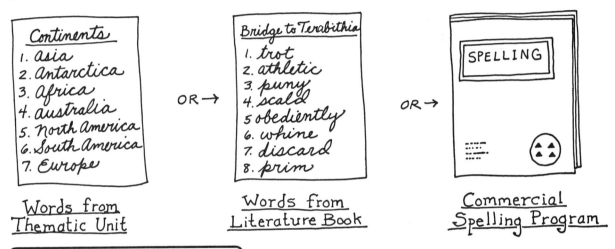

Continents	Bridge to Terabithia	SPELLING
Words from Thematic Unit	Words from Literature Book	Commercial Spelling Program

SENTENCES/PARAGRAPHS

Write Original Paragraphs
Fluent writers no longer need story frames to help them structure their writing. They have mastered the writing process sufficiently to apply skills in a more direct and holistic way. These sample exercises can be used as individual journal assignments, but are most effective when used as extensions of thematic units.

Sample Thematic Unit	Sample Paragraph Assignment
The Human Body	Write a paragraph as if you were a system of the human body. What do you do?
Earthquakes/Volcanoes	Describe an earthquake or volcanic eruption as a news announcer would.
Pioneers/Westward Movement	Pretend you are a pioneer. Describe your trip west and explain why you took it.

Use Vivid Words (Adjectives/Adverbs/Verbs)

Fluent learners can practice using vivid words when writing paragraphs or journal assignments. Exercises which promote this skill should be based on thematic units currently being studied.

<u>Read/Discuss Vivid Words</u>
Students hear or read vivid word passage and discuss it.

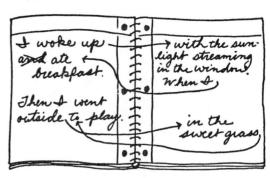

<u>Revise Writing with Vivid Words</u>
Students revise a journal or writing assignment they have already done by injecting vivid words.

Capitalization/Punctuation/Grammar

The elements of capitalization, punctuation, and grammar are important to fluent learners' writing; however, fluent learners should be more concerned with the content of their writing assignments than with the mechanics. It is important, then, that these skills become second nature to the fluent writer, and with constant practice, they will!

Appropriate skills for fluent writers are:

Capitalization	– Proper Nouns
	– Book Titles
Punctuation	– . ? ! , : " "
Grammar	– can/may, lay/lie/laid
	– I/me
	– subject/verb agreement

Students are not able to internalize these skills through the use of worksheets. Only real writing experiences will do that. Once a skill is taught, therefore, students should apply it often in their writing. Teachers should correct only for the specific skill being practiced when grading these assignments.

Quotation Marks

She said, "Hi Mandy, what cha doin'?"
"Not much," Mandy said. "I just went to the store for a soda."
"Great!" said Sue. "I'll have one too."

104

Letter Form (Personal/Business)

Fluent learners should be taught the correct format for personal and business letters. While the personal letter format most likely will have been previously introduced, the business letter format should be new to most fluent learners.

<u>Personal Letters</u>

- pen pals
- answer younger, emergent-learner letters to Santa Claus, Easter Bunny, Leprauchans, etc.

<u>Business Letters</u>

- gather information for reports (state or country reports).
- write to people/agencies expressing an opinion (U.N. to save rainforests, etc.)

Poetry

Fluent writers should be hearing and reading poetry on a regular basis. Rhyming poems should not be the only style of poetry read or written. Other types of poems appropriate for fluent writers include:

<u>Haiku</u>

(5 syllables) Spring buds burst open.
(7 syllables) Crooked brown branches give life
(5 syllables) to summer's color.

<u>Cinquain</u>

Flower   (one word title)
lacy, pink   (two adjectives)
sprouting, budding, blooming   (three action verbs)
beautiful in the morning   (four words expressing a feeling about title.)
Hyacinth   (synonym)

<u>Limerick</u>
(write for the rythm of the words)

There was a young kitten from camp
   who scrambled away from the damp.
When a break in the hose
   sprinkled her nose,
She handled it just like a champ.

<u>Picture Poetry</u>

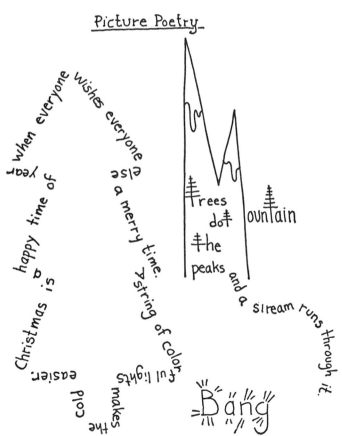

105

Organize Information for Paragraph/Reports

Learning how to organize information for paragraphs and reports is one of the most crucial skills for fluent writers, especially older students in fifth or sixth grades. Organization is an essential skill for writing the reports and longer exercises required in these grades.

Semantic mapping is one of the best and easiest way to organize ideas for both paragraph and report writing.

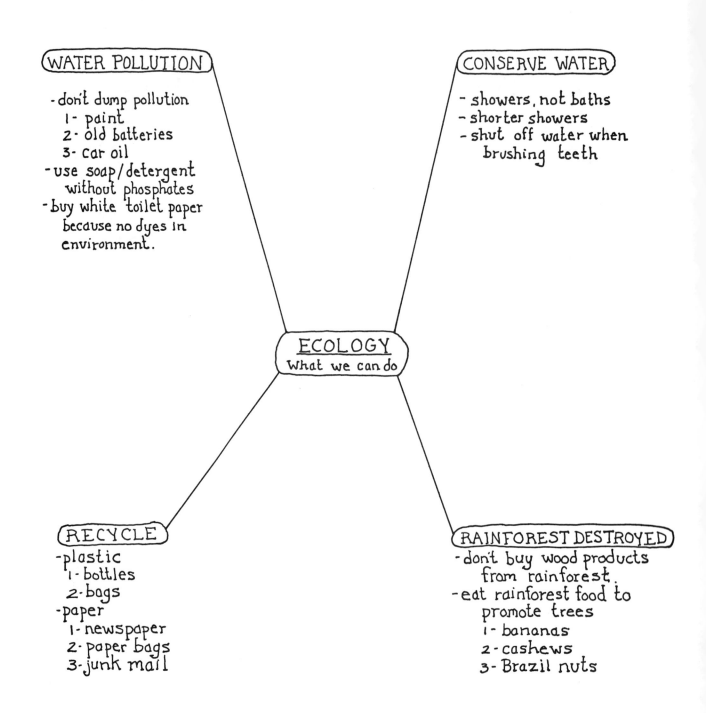

WATER POLLUTION

- don't dump pollution
  1 - paint
  2 - old batteries
  3 - car oil
- use soap/detergent without phosphates
- buy white toilet paper because no dyes in environment.

CONSERVE WATER

- showers, not baths
- shorter showers
- shut off water when brushing teeth

ECOLOGY
What we can do

RECYCLE
- plastic
  1 - bottles
  2 - bags
- paper
  1 - newspaper
  2 - paper bags
  3 - junk mail

RAINFOREST DESTROYED
- don't buy wood products from rainforest.
- eat rainforest food to promote trees
  1 - bananas
  2 - cashews
  3 - Brazil nuts

At the culmination of a thematic unit, fluent writers can be expected to synthesize all of the information they have learned and write a cohesive summarizing paragraph:

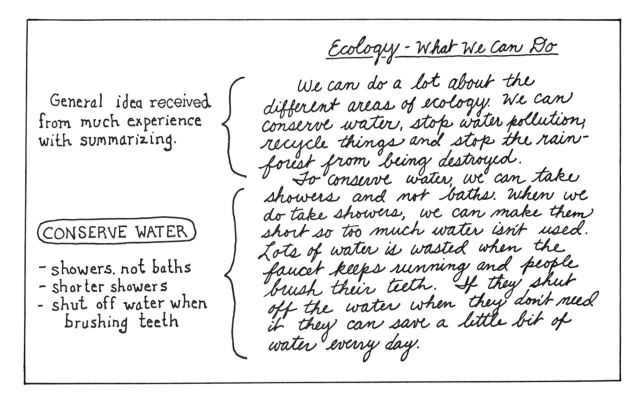

General idea received from much experience with summarizing.

CONSERVE WATER

- showers, not baths
- shorter showers
- shut off water when brushing teeth

Ecology - What We Can Do

We can do a lot about the different areas of ecology. We can conserve water, stop water pollution, recycle things and stop the rainforest from being destroyed.

To conserve water, we can take showers and not baths. When we do take showers, we can make them short so too much water isn't used. Lots of water is wasted when the faucet keeps running and people brush their teeth. If they shut off the water when they don't need it they can save a little bit of water every day.

The idea behind organizing is to place information in such a way that it can be used effectively by the writer, and semantic mapping is an ideal tool as it is often better understood by elementary and middle school children than is the traditional outline.

107

Chapter Nine

LESSON PLANS AND THEMATIC UNITS

In whole language instruction, lesson plans are based on thematic units. A theme makes daily planning manageable by providing a focal point for both the teacher and the students. When each activity relates to a central theme, students are better able to comprehend and internalize the information they are learning.

Lesson should not be over-planned or designed to be too creative for students who aren't ready to employ advanced independent thinking skills. If the teacher plans too many innovative activities, young students may sometimes lose sight of the central theme being studied and become confused. This is best avoided by concentrating on the major concepts of the theme being studied. Students learn best when they clearly see the connection between each activity and the theme to which it relates.

MAKE PLANNING MANAGEABLE

In order to create a thematic-based lesson plan that will not be overwhelming in scope or size, keep a few simple principles in mind:
1. Include any district mandated themes.
2. Decide on concepts to be developed.
3. Choose literature books to support those concepts.
4. Base reading, writing, listening, and speaking activities on those concepts.
5. Incorporate activities and ideas already on hand or commercially available.

The teaching day should be thought of as a whole unit and not as divided by separate subjects. All activities should focus on one or more daily concept and employ all the attributes of good lesson design and grouping previously discussed.

Appropriate thematic units for each grade and developmental level are provided (page 109). Examples of a week's thematic lesson plan for each developmental level and a blank planning sheet are presented on pages 110 through 119. These lessons are meant to serve only as examples, as most thematic units of study will last longer than one week.

EMERGENT LEARNERS

Grade K:
- All About Me
- My Body
- Health/Nutrition
- My Family/Home
- Seasons
- Self-esteem
- Nursery Rhymes
- Holidays Around the World
- Community Helpers
- Animals (zoo, farm, etc.)
- Fairy Tales
- Five Senses

Grade 1:
- My Home/Family
- Self-esteem
- Community Helpers
- Map Skills
- Native Americans
- Sea Life
- Animals/Habitats
- Celebrations Around the World
- My Body (dental health)
- Plants
- Weather/Seasons
- Fairy Tales/Poetry

DEVELOPING LEARNERS

Grade 2:
- Map Skills
- Multicultural Education
- African Americans
- Native Americans
- Asian Americans
- My Family/Home
- Community Helpers
- Fairy and Folk Tales
- Food Groups/Pyramid
- Weather
- Plants
- Health
- Environment/Ecology
- Animals/Habitats (adaptability)
- Sea Life (sharks, etc.)
- Poetry

Grade 3:
- Geography
- Map Skills/Globe
- Our Country
- Multicultural Education
- Indians/Pilgrims
- Folk Tales/Poetry/Fables
- Insects
- Dinosaurs
- Solar System
- Ecology
- Rocks/Minerals
- Animals/Habitats (land/sea)

FLUENT LEARNERS

Grade 4:
- State History
- Geography/Maps/Globe
- Feelings/Emotions
- My Family History
- Fables/Legends/Poetry
- Flight/Machines
- Animal Kingdom (predator/prey)
- Human Body
- Earthquakes/Volcanos
- Ecology
- Magnets/Electricity
- Appreciating other cultures as well as our own

Grade 5:
- American History
- Colonies
- Westward Movement
- Civil War
- Industrial Revolution
- North American Neighbors
- Map/Globe Skills
- Plants
- Animals (endangered species)
- Solar System (universe/rockets)
- Human Body
- Ecology
- Historical Fiction
- Autobiographies/Poetry

Grade 6:
- Ancient Civilizations
- Geography/Maps
- The World
- Cultures/Food
- Celebrations
- Geology
- Ecology/Environment
- Human Body
- Mythology
- Contemporary Novels/Short Stories/Poetry

While many themes are repeated from grade to grade and level to level, the concepts developed in them differ.

Sample Thematic Unit: ALL ABOUT ME

MONDAY	TUESDAY	WEDNESDAY	THURSDAY	FRIDAY
Concept: I Am Special	Concept: Growing/Changing	Concept: We Have Feelings	Concept: Families	Concept: Friendship
READ ALOUD: *Chrysanthemum* by Kevin Henkes	**READ ALOUD:** *Leo the Late Bloomer* by Robert Kraus	**READ ALOUD:** *Alexander and the Terrible, Horrible, No Good, Very Bad Day* by Judith Viorst	**READ ALOUD:** *What Kind of Family Do You Have?* by Gretchen Super	**READ ALOUD:** *Will You Be My Friend?* by Eric Carle
WRITING: • Complete sentence frame: "I like my name because _____." Illustrate.	**WRITING:** • Complete sentence frame: "Before I couldn't ____. Now I can." Illustrate.	**WRITING:** • Draw/write chain of a very bad day.	**WRITING:** • Complete sentence frame: "My family is _____."	**WRITING:** • Complete sentence frame: "My friend is _____."
READING EXPERIENCE: *Chrysanthemum* – Henkes • Group: Sequence story events. Conferences/observation	**READING EXPERIENCE:** *Leo the Late Bloomer* – Kraus • Group: Story Frame Character / Problem / Solution Conferences/observation	**READING EXPERIENCE:** *Alexander … Bad Day* – Viorst • Group: Chart story. "My Terrific, … Very Good Day." Work on antonyms. Conferences/observation	**READING EXPERIENCE:** *What Kind of Family* – Super • Group: Pocket chart/family words: "My family has ____ people. A ____, ____." Conferences/observation	**ACTIVITY CHOICES:** • "All About Me" mobile. • "How I Feel" toast. (Use peanut butter & raisins.) Conferences/observation
• Listening: *Proud To Be Me* – Lisa Anderson • Seatwork Activities: – Write full name and decorate it. – Draw/write special things about self.	• Listening: *How Tall Are You?* – JoAnne Nelson • Seatwork Activities: – Paired reading. – Draw/write things you can/can't do. Share with friend.	• Listening: *I Have Feelings* – Terry Berger • Seatwork Activities: – Act out story. – Draw/write examples of antonyms.	• Listening: *Helping Out* – George Ancona • Seatwork Activities: – Manipulate pocket chart words/phrases. – Draw/write each family member. Cut out for math.	• Listening: *Frederick and His Friends* – Lionni • Act out: Act out things to do with friends. • Body outline: Draw body outline on butcher paper. Color.
MATH: • Shortest/longest: Number of letters in students' names. Graph results.	**MATH:** • Count/write numbers as far as you can. Compare to what had been done earlier.	**MATH:** • Categorizing: things that make you feel happy/sad/angry/sleepy, etc.	**MATH:** • Story problems: Count and manipulate pictures of family members.	
LUNCH	**LUNCH**	**LUNCH**	**LUNCH**	**LUNCH**
READ ALOUD: *We Are All Alike, We Are All Different* – Cheltenham Elem. School Kindergarten	**READ ALOUD:** *Things I Can Do Myself* – Craig Lovik	**READ ALOUD:** *Harry and the Terrible Whatzit* – Dick Gackenbach	**READ ALOUD:** *The Terrible Thing That Happened At Our House* – Marge Blaine	**READ ALOUD:** *Chester's Way* – Kevin Henkes
SCIENCE: • Write/discuss how children are same and different.	**SCIENCE:** • Discussion: "Growing Up: How I've Changed." Tell partners.	**SCIENCE:** • Feelings are natural, not good or bad. List different feelings & compare them.	**SCIENCE:** • Different kinds of families– animals & people & how they help each other.	**CULMINATING ACTIVITIES**
SOCIAL STUDIES: • Poster: Cut and paste magazine pictures of things you like.	**SOCIAL STUDIES:** • Time line: Important events in your life.	**SOCIAL STUDIES:** • Act out ways to deal with different feelings: anger, fear, sadness, love, etc.	**SOCIAL STUDIES:** • Families are people who love you. List/draw things children do to help family.	**SCIENCE:** • "Taking Care of Me"
FINE ARTS: • Homework bracelet: "How I Got My Name."	**FINE ARTS:** • Design award for something new you can do.	**FINE ARTS:** • Dance/pantomime different feelings.	**FINE ARTS:** • Triarama: "My Family"	**SOCIAL STUDIES:** • Evaluation: "What I Learned About Me"
				FINE ARTS: • Folder for week's work. • Share/perform morning's activities.
SILENT READING	**SILENT READING**	**SILENT READING**	**SILENT READING**	**SILENT READING**
P. E.	**P. E.**	**P. E.**	**P. E.**	**P. E.**

RELATED MATERIALS

WORDS TO LEARN:
family, mother, father, sister, brother, grandma, grandpa, feelings, friends, happy, sad, love, mad

RELATED BOOKS:
Don't Feed the Monsters on Tuesdays – Adolph Moser
Stevie – John Steptoe
Feelings – Aliki
Love You Forever – Robert Munsch
I'll Fix Anthony – Judith Viorst
Ira Sleeps Over – Bernard Waber
The Friendship Factor – William Coleman
Families Are Friends – Harper, S.F.

RELATED ACTIVITIES:
• Principal explains about his or her family/friends.
• Older students discuss options to fighting when mad.

Thematic Unit: All About Me

The concepts in this thematic unit change daily. The books to be read aloud reinforce each day's concept, making it easier for the student as well as the teacher to focus attention on a single idea. It is assumed that good lesson design will be employed to fully develop each area of the curriculum for optimum learning.

Read Aloud: The teacher reads aloud at least twice a day. Writing, math, science, social studies, and fine arts activities are all based on this reading.

Writing: Emergent children need a great deal of experience brainstorming ideas from topics the teacher writes either on the board, on chart paper, or on sentence strips for a pocket chart. When using sentence frames, the same activities apply. The teacher writes the sentence frame on the board and encourages children to provide words, phrases, and ideas which complete it. The teacher should always reread the sentence frame, pointing to each word as it is read aloud. When it is time to write, the students should be so full of ideas that they can't wait to write and illustrate their work.

Reading Experience: An effective technique when working with reading comprehension concepts is to divide children into groups. This allows students to receive more individualized attention. While one group works on reading comprehension skills, other groups can be involved in a Listening Activity or one of the Seatwork Activities.

Group: The teacher rereads the story. If big books of the story are available, the teacher should point to each word as it is read aloud and encourage children to read along. The teacher should then explain the concept step-by-step and discuss with the students how to sequence events, and use a story frame or story problem. Students should be encouraged to talk about their comprehension processes as well. Only by making children aware of the comprehension process will they understand how to apply it for themselves.

Listening: All children take turns in the listening center and listen to a story either at the listening post, from another adult, or from an older child reading aloud.

Seatwork Activities: One or more of these activities are to be completed by each student. When students are ready, they can either read a book, write at the writing center, or choose from other whole language activities routinely available.

Friday Activity Choices: These are culminating activities that reinforce the thematic concepts taught during the week. These activities should employ all aspects of whole language—listening, speaking, reading, and writing. Children choose the activities they want to complete, thus forming heterogeneous interest groups (an example of flexible grouping).

Math: Math activities utilize basic skills. The concepts of shortest/longest, graphing, writing numbers, categorizing, and story problems are covered in the context of the day's concept.

Lunch

Read Aloud: The teacher reads aloud again and derives science, social studies, and fine arts activities from the book.

Science: Science concepts for emergent learners should first be related to the students themselves and then be expanded upon. Children internalize and retain information best when they connect ideas to personal experiences.

Social Studies: All social studies activities are related to the students' lives. No value judgments are to be made when dealing with concepts of self-esteem. The main ideas enforced are that everyone is special and unique, feelings are natural (not good or bad), and families and friends come in all shapes and sizes.

Fine Arts: Fine arts consists of both the visual and performing arts, and students should complete activities in both areas. Music, poems, finger plays, dancing, pantomimes, plays, and puppet shows should constitute a part of the day. Through these experiences young children learn by applying their knowledge in ways their writing skills are not developed enough to allow them to do.

Silent Reading (5-15 minutes): Plenty of books relating to the theme being studied should be available to the students. Children can explore these books during the silent reading period.

P.E.

Dismissal

Sample Thematic Unit: INSECTS

MONDAY	TUESDAY	WEDNESDAY	THURSDAY	FRIDAY
Concept: Insect Parts	Concept: Types of Insects	Concept: Insect Life Cycle	Concept: Camouflage/Defense	Concept: Honeybees
READ ALOUD: *Two Bad Ants* – Chris Van Allsburg	**READ ALOUD:** *Icky Bug Alphabet Book* – Jerry Pallotta	**READ ALOUD:** *Where Butterflies Grow* – Joanna Ryder	**READ ALOUD:** *How To Hide a Butterfly* – Ruth Heller	**READ ALOUD:** *The World of Honeybees* – Virginia Harrison
WRITING: • Describe something from an ant's point of view.	**WRITING:** • Write about an insect you like or don't like. Tell why.	**WRITING:** • Describe place you would want to grow as butterfly. Use vivid words.	**WRITING:** • Write poems about favorite insects.	**WRITING:** • "My Day As A Honeybee"
READING EXPERIENCE: *Two Bad Ants* – Allsburg • Group: Summarize/sequence flipbook: beginning/middle/end Conferences/observation • Listening: *Insects That Live in Families* – Dean Morris • Seatwork Activities: –Paired reading. –Write small group story: "Two Good Ants."	**READING EXPERIENCE:** *Icky Bug Book* – Pallotta • Group: Compare/contrast two insects from book. Conferences/observation • Listening: *Beetles Lightly Toasted* – Phyllis Reynolds-Taylor • Seatwork Activities: –Gather information about favorite insect. – Begin insect ABC book.	**READING EXPERIENCE:** *Where Butterflies Grow* – Ryder • Group: Sequence life cycle of butterfly Conferences/observation • Listening: *Insects in Winter* – Millicent Selsam • Seatwork Activities: –Write/draw butterfly life cycle. –Continue ABC book.	**READING EXPERIENCE:** *How To Hide a Butterfly* – Heller • Group: Predict outcomes: Chain what might happen if no defenses in insects. Conferences/observation • Listening: *Amazing Fact Book of Insects* – Horton, et.al. • Seatwork Activities: –Paired reading. –Continue work on ABC book.	**ACTIVITY CHOICES:** • Cook with honey (peanut butter/honey balls) Conferences/observation • Listening: *When Woods Hum* – Joanna Ryder • Observation Station: Observe/draw insects. • Puppets: Act out insect behavior with insect puppets. • Mural/ABC books: Continue work on these.
MATH: • Count/write by 3's OR • Introduce multiplying by 3.	**MATH:** • Insect walk: Graph types of insects seen on insect walk.	**MATH:** • Measurement/time: Calculate how far mealy bugs travel in 30 seconds; in an hour.	**MATH:** • Insect problem-solving.	
LUNCH	LUNCH	LUNCH	LUNCH	LUNCH
READ ALOUD: *Ant Cities* – Arthur Dorros	**READ ALOUD:** *Billions of Bugs* – Harris Petrie	**READ ALOUD:** *Diary of a Monarch Butterfly* – Susan Thompson	**READ ALOUD:** *Find the Hidden Insect* – Joanna Cole	**READ ALOUD:** *The World of Honeybees* – Harrison
SCIENCE: • Insects have 3 body parts, 6 legs: head/thorax/abdomen. Cut/paste insect parts.	**SCIENCE:** • Make insect observation station • Observe/record insect behavior in pairs/small groups	**SCIENCE:** • Discuss and compare/contrast the life cycles of a moth/fly/butterfly. Draw them.	**SCIENCE:** • Types of defense mechanisms: –taste bad –mimic other bug –hide/camouflage –size/sound (mantis hiss)	**CULMINATING ACTIVITIES** **SCIENCE:** • Perform insect puppet show. • Share insect observations.
SOCIAL STUDIES: • Ants work in colonies; how are we the same? • Make an ant farm.	**SOCIAL STUDIES:** • Helpful/harmful insects. In small groups: Brainstorm how to control harmful insects and boost helpful ones?	**SOCIAL STUDIES:** • Map monarch butterfly migration.	**SOCIAL STUDIES:** • If you were a bird, which insect would you eat? Why?	**SOCIAL STUDIES:** • Discuss feelings about insects now. • How bees helpful/necessary.
FINE ARTS: • Cover for insect folder. • Thumbprint ants.	**FINE ARTS:** • Clay/pipe cleaners: design own insect, explain to small group	**FINE ARTS:** • Act out life cycles of insects. • Begin insect mural.	**FINE ARTS:** • Draw/paint camouflaged insects. Paste on mural.	**FINE ARTS:** • Finish/share ABC books. • Finish/share class mural.
SILENT READING	SILENT READING	SILENT READING	SILENT READING	SILENT READING
P. E.	P. E.	P. E.	P. E.	P. E.

RELATED MATERIALS

SPELLING WORDS:

1. insect
2. thorax
3. head
4. abdomen
5. six legs
6. butterfly
7. caterpillar
8. chrysalis
9. cocoon
10. larva

RELATED BOOKS:

The Very Quiet Cricket – Eric Carle

Creepy Crawly Critter Riddles – Joanne Bernstein

I Wish I Were a Butterfly – James Howe

Backyard Insects – Millicent Selsam

When It Comes To Bugs – Aileen Fisher

Insects Do the Strangest Things – Leonora Hornblow

Bugs: Poems – Mary Ann Hoberman

RELATED ACTIVITIES:

• Grow silkworms.
• Farmer speaks on pest control.
• Share insect collection or bring insects to class.

Thematic Unit: Insects

Each day of the developing learner's thematic unit is based on a particular concept, and a variety of books are used to reinforce each concept. Other books can be substituted or added if the teacher wishes.

Read Aloud: Two Read Aloud units are scheduled per day. As previously discussed, this important activity builds student success in reading and adds the much-needed dimension of listening to the whole language program.

Writing: In journals, children write their responses to an aspect of the story they heard read aloud. The teacher reads the students' journals for ideas and not spelling and punctuation errors.

Reading Experience: The students follow the Read Aloud story with activities, and are then asked to reread the story with an eye for specific comprehension tasks.

> *Group:* These activities can be used with reading groups of all ability levels or in a whole group set-up.

> *Listening:* All children listen to a related book at the listening post, one group at a time.

> *Seatwork Activities:* Students complete one or all of the seatwork activities. These are to be completed in individual, pairs, or small group situations to provide students with a variety of grouping experiences.

> *Friday Activity Choices:* These activities culminate the themes discussed during the entire week and apply the students' knowledge in meaningful ways. They should involve all aspects of whole language—listening, speaking, reading, and writing.

Math: Lessons in basic math skills such as counting by 3's, graphing, measurement, and problem-solving should be designed to reinforce each day's thematic concept.

Lunch

Read Aloud: The teacher reads aloud a different book that reinforces the daily concept. Science, social studies, and fine arts activities are derived from the book read.

Science: Lessons conducted in individual and small group situations reinforce basic concepts learned about insects. Observation is an important aspect of science investigation; numerous hands-on experiences should be provided. Many of the suggested activities can be used in connection with the study of social studies and fine arts.

Social Studies: Many comparisons are drawn between insects and people. These activities stimulate critical thinking and surpass the simple knowledge of basic facts by applying what is being learned to new situations. Many group activities strengthen students' ideas.

Fine Arts: Developing learners should be exposed to the study of both visual and performing arts. Supply a variety of material for visual art production as well as opportunities to perform in small or large groups.

Silent Reading (15-25 minutes): Children choose books associated with insects for silent reading.

P.E.

Dismissal

Sample Thematic Unit: NATIVE AMERICANS/SURVIVAL

MONDAY	TUESDAY	WEDNESDAY	THURSDAY	FRIDAY
READ ALOUD: Ch. 1, *Island of the Blue Dolphins* – Scott O'Dell	**READ ALOUD:** Ch. 4, *Island . . . Dolphins*	**READ ALOUD:** Ch. 7, *Island . . . Dolphins*	**READ ALOUD:** Ch. 10, *Island . . . Dolphins*	**READ ALOUD:** Ch. 13, *Island . . . Dolphins*
WRITING: • Invent a secret name for yourself and explain it.	**WRITING:** • Rewrite ch. 4 from Captain Orlov's point of view.	**WRITING:** • What would you do in Karana's situation? Why?	**WRITING:** • What might have happened if Karana had continued in the canoe?	**WRITING:** • Write what you know about sea elephants.
READING EXPERIENCE: Ch. 2, *Island . . . Dolphins* • Group: Was it right for Chief Chowig to not share? Why? Why not? What might happen as a result? • Conferences/observation • Listening: Teacher retells chs. 1–2 from Karana's point of view. • Seatwork Activities: –Draw map of island. –Tape record chs. 3–5. –Write a fair agreement between Capt. Orlov and Chief Chowig.	**READING EXPERIENCE:** Ch. 5, *Island . . . Dolphins* • Group: Skim chapter for Kimiki's decision. Discuss how else problem could have been solved. • Conferences/observation • Listening: Reading group retells chs. 3–5 from Karana's point of view. • Seatwork Activities: –Write items you would pack if you were Kimiki. –Tape record chs. 6–8. –Flipbook: Village before and after battle.	**READING EXPERIENCE:** Ch. 8, *Island . . . Dolphins* • Group: Read chapter for major events. Summarize. • Conferences/observation • Listening: Reading group retells chs. 6–8 from Karana's point of view. • Seatwork Activities: –Plan burial ceremony for Remo. –Tape record chs. 9–11. –Chain how you would react to wild dogs.	**READING EXPERIENCE:** Ch. 11, *Island . . . Dolphins* • Group: Explain Karana's change of heart. Give new title to chp. Explain why. • Conferences/observation • Listening: Reading group retells chs. 9–11 from Karana's point of view. • Seatwork Activities: –Design a survival shelter with fence. –Tape record chs. 12–13. –Write a diary entry for Karana.	**ACTIVITY CHOICES:** • Diarama: Make a diarama of Karana's home. Label/explain parts. • Conferences/observation • Listening: Chs. 12–13, *Island . . . Dolphins* • Weave a basket and tell what you would put in it. • Invent a legend explaining how dolphins came to be known as good omens. • Construct model of a canoe; explain what you would pack on a canoe trip and why.
MATH: • Measurement: Convert leagues into feet, yards, and miles.	**MATH:** • Problem-solving: How would you divide work among 8 women and 7 old men?	**MATH:** • In pairs, make up 3 multiplication and 3 division problems from story events. Exchange & solve.	**MATH:** • In small groups, calculate how long Karana has been on island by end of chp. 11.	**LUNCH**
LUNCH	**LUNCH**	**LUNCH**	**LUNCH**	**READ ALOUD:** Ch. 14, *Island . . . Dolphins*
READ ALOUD: Ch. 3, *Island . . . Dolphins*	**READ ALOUD:** Ch. 6, *Island . . . Dolphins*	**READ ALOUD:** Ch. 9, *Island . . . Dolphins*	**READ ALOUD:** Ch. 12, *Island . . . Dolphins*	**CULMINATING ACTIVITIES**
SCIENCE: • Compare/contrast sea otters and seals.	**SCIENCE:** • Life in kelp beds. • Kelp forests.	**SCIENCE:** • Discuss parts of shellfish. • Dissect a shellfish.	**SCIENCE:** • Sea elephants –habitat –food/behavior	**SCIENCE:** • Discuss why and how Karana's first aid techniques were helpful.
SOCIAL STUDIES: • In small groups, discuss Karana's tribe.	**SOCIAL STUDIES:** • Discuss reactions to leaving island on white man's ship.	**SOCIAL STUDIES:** • In small groups discuss why women weren't allowed to make weapons.	**SOCIAL STUDIES:** • Basic survival techniques & how Karana used them.	**SOCIAL STUDIES:** • In small groups, discuss the decision to build two shelters. Was it a good or bad decision? Why?
FINE ARTS: • Map islands of southern California.	**FINE ARTS:** • Triarama of ship scene.	**FINE ARTS:** • Act out a scene in which men explain why women weren't allowed to make weapons.	**FINE ARTS:** • Clay: Fashion 2 utensils and explain why they were chosen.	**FINE ARTS:** • Share projects completed during the morning.
SILENT READING	**SILENT READING**	**SILENT READING**	**SILENT READING**	**SILENT READING**
P. E.	**P. E.**	**P. E.**	**P. E.**	**P. E.**

RELATED MATERIALS

SPELLING WORDS:

1. kelp
2. pelt
3. abalone
4. sea elephant
5. ancestors
6. sinew
7. trinkets
8. crevice
9. omen
10. rites
11. lair
12. carcass
13. otter
14. seal
15. dolphin

RELATED BOOKS:

The Cay – Theodore Taylor

Hatchet – Gary Paulsen

Call It Courage – Armstrong Perry

Flyaway – Lynn Hall

Sign of the Beaver – Elizabeth George Speare

Julie of the Wolves – Jean Craighead George

Willy Whitefeather's Outdoor Survival Handbook for Kids – Willy Whitefeather

RELATED ACTIVITIES:

• Mountaineering expert on survival techniques.
• Basket weaving.
• Taste fish mentioned in the story.

Thematic Unit: Native Americans/Survival

This course of study for fluent learners is based the book *Island of the Blue Dolphins* by Scott O'Dell, which tells the true story of an isolated Native American living on one of the Channel Islands off the coast of southern California. In addition to Native American customs and survival techniques, many other skills and concepts are incorporated into this unit. This week's lesson plan is simply a sketch to illustrate how to employ the many facets of whole language instruction outlined in previous chapters.

Read Aloud: *Island of the Blue Dolphins* is studied by being both read aloud by the teacher and read silently by students.

Writing: Students react to an aspect of the chapter read aloud.

Reading Experience: It is assumed the teacher will be either meeting with more than one reading group or with the class as a whole while studying *Island of the Blue Dolphins*. Every student will participate in a daily Listening Activity as well as one of the Seatwork Activities.

Group: Reads chapters in *Island of the Blue Dolphins*.

Listening: The teacher records a retelling of events in Chapters 1 and 2 from the main character's (Karana) point of view, using voice inflection and sound effects, if possible. This will serve as a model for student recordings throughout the week.

Seatwork Activities: Students are assigned to complete one or more of these activities. Different reading groups are assigned to read three chapters of the story and retell it from Karana's point of view on the tape recorder for the next day's listening experience. Students should be encouraged to make use of sound effects, vivid words, and voice inflection.

Friday Activity Choices: These activities synthesize the information students have learned during the week and apply the knowledge they have gained in real ways. These activities should employ all aspects of whole language—listening, speaking, reading, and writing.

Math: Math lessons are conducted most often in a whole group set-up. Appropriate math concepts include converting units of measurement, problem-solving, and applying math to the story. It may be necessary to reinforce selected concepts with lessons conducted in small groups.

Lunch

Read Aloud: The teacher reads another chapter aloud from which science, social studies, and fine arts activities are derived. By the end of each day, three chapters of *Island of the Blue Dolphins* will have been read and studied.

Science: Science experiences related to the study of marine animals used by Native Americans for food and tools are derived from the book.

Social Studies: Native American lifestyle and survival techniques are studied by relating them to students' own reactions and beliefs. Many small group situations encourage productive brainstorming sessions and the application of higher level thinking skills.

Fine Arts: Students are introduced to both the visual and performing arts. The teacher should make available a variety of supplies for projects. Role-playing and shared or group projects should also be introduced to the week's activities.

Silent Reading (25-35 minutes): Students read related books or books by the same author during this time.

P.E.

Dismissal

Thematic Unit: PLANNING SHEET

	MONDAY	TUESDAY	WEDNESDAY	THURSDAY	FRIDAY
READ ALOUD:					
WRITING:					
READING EXPERIENCE: •Group:					ACTIVITY CHOICES:
Conferences/observation •Listening:					Conferences/observation •Listening:
•Seatwork Activities:					
MATH:					
LUNCH					LUNCH
READ ALOUD:					READ ALOUD:
SCIENCE:					CULMINATING ACTIVITIES SCIENCE:
SOCIAL STUDIES:					
FINE ARTS:					
SILENT READING P. E.					

RELATED MATERIALS

Chapter Ten

EVALUATION

How can a whole language program be evaluated? Ideas for effective whole language evaluation are being tested at all levels of education—in the classroom, the school, the district, the state, and nationally. For the first time since standardized testing became the norm, test-makers are seriously reconsidering the best way to assess learning. Even the nation's largest producers of standardized tests are looking for ways to change their methods. This constitutes a major shift of emphasis away from the standard multiple-choice format to what is known as performance assessment.

PERFORMANCE ASSESSMENT vs. STANDARDIZED TESTS

In the past, federal programs, states, districts, and parents were only interested in the type of assessment provided by standardized tests. These tests provide norm-referenced data about how students at various grade levels rate when compared with similar students nationwide. The information that such evaluations provide is still useful and should not be disregarded; however, total reliance on these tests provides a limited picture of a student's thinking process.

Since the release of the landmark study *Becoming A Nation of Readers,* which recommends the type of whole language instruction children require, there has been a wider recognition of the need for evaluations that assess the complexities of student learning. This goal can be accomplished only by using real activities that mirror those of the classroom. This new type of test is called a performance assessment.

There are a number of ways a child's performance and thinking processes can be assessed. They include:
- informal activities
- portfolios
- observation/anecdotal records
- conferences
- integrated performance assessment
- standardized tests

Maintaining a good balance among all of these methods will provide the most thorough assessment of a child's success in a whole language program.

INFORMAL ASSESSMENT

These are quick assessments that take only ten to fifteen minutes to administer and that communicate a sense of which skills students have mastered and in which areas they still need to work. This form of assessment provides an excellent way for teachers to decide which of their students to place in a flexible group in order to re-examine a particular concept. Informal assessments can be administered approximately once a week.

To administer informal assessments, students are given either lined or unlined paper and instructed how to fold the paper. They then number the boxes and perform teacher-directed tasks in each box.

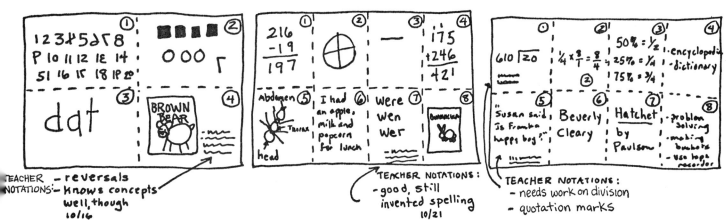

TEACHER NOTATIONS: – reversals – knows concepts well, though 10/16

TEACHER NOTATIONS: – good, still invented spelling 10/21

TEACHER NOTATIONS: – needs work on division – quotation marks

EMERGENT (gds K-1)	DEVELOPING (gds 2-3)	FLUENT (gds 4-6)

EMERGENT (gds K-1)

Example: (4 or 8 boxes used)

Box #1 · Write numbers to 20.

#2 · Draw 4 squares. Draw 3 circles How many altogether?

#3 · Write "bat"

#4 · Draw or write about ___ your favorite book ___

#5 · Write this math problem and solve it: "Three plus seven equals"

#6 · Draw and write your favorite part of the "All about Me" unit.

#7 · Write and punctuate this sentence: "A cat is hot."

#8 · What are your two favorite things to do in school?

DEVELOPING (gds 2-3)

Example:

Box #1 · Do this: $\frac{216}{-19}$

#2 · Draw a circle divided into fourths.

#3 · Draw a line about two inches long.

#4 · Do this: 175 + 246 =

#5 · Draw an insect. Label the parts.

#6 · Write/punctuate this sentence "I had an apple, milk, and popcorn for lunch.

#7 · Write these words: where · when · were.

#8 · Write/draw the title and author of your favorite book.

FLUENT (gds 4-6)

Example:

Box #1 · Write and do this math: 20⟌610

#2 · ¼ of 8 ?

#3 · What % = ½, ¼, ¾, ?

#4 · List sources which provide information about camels.

#5 · Write/punctuate this sentence: Susan said, "Is Frank a happy boy?"

#6 · Who is your favorite author?

#7 · What is the title of the book you are reading? The author?

#8 · Write your three favorite things you learned when we studied Island of the Blue Dolphins.

121

Math concepts, spelling and punctuation, thematic unit specifics, study skills, and even reactions to books and activities can be evaluated with the informal assessment. These activities are not meant to be corrected and handed back to the children. A teacher can simply mark the skills that still need work, date the paper, and place it in a child's portfolio. This provides a good sampling of concepts for parents to see and note improvements.

Teacher assesses and notes child's skills on paper for conferencing.

Becomes part of portfolio shown to student/parents on conference day.

PORTFOLIOS

Portfolios of students' work best illustrate the learning students have gained over the year and provide a great format for parents and teachers, as well as children, to chart their progress. Portfolios are nothing more than folders containing samples of students' work. It is best to maintain two or three folders for different types of work. The folders can contain:

- samples of math papers, reports, etc.
- audio tapes of a child's reading-aloud skills
- writing journals, reading logs, thematic projects, etc.
- anecdotal records compiled by the teacher
- informal assessments

Student-/teacher-chosen work should include different subjects each week.

Audio tapes of child reading aloud or retelling a story once a month.

Writing journals, reading logs, reports, thematic projects.

Informal Assessments
Should be included with anecdotal records.

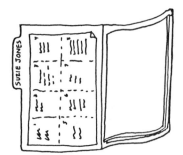

Anecdotal Records
Teacher makes during conferences or observation.

Portfolios should be manageable and not create stress for either teachers or students. Portfolio samples can be sent home to parents once a week. Teachers can either direct the children to select work samples from one or two subject areas, or choose some themselves. As a rule, samples from each subject area should be placed in portfolios once every three or four weeks; however, children should feel free to add special papers if they wish. In addition to student work, anecdotal records kept by the teacher should be in a separate portfolio.

OBSERVATION/ANECDOTAL RECORDS

This form of assessment should be a comfortable and manageable part of every whole language program. Time can be reserved each day for teachers to informally observe their students and write anecdotal notes about their activities. This not only keeps teachers apprised of those students on task or having difficulty, but it provides an opportunity to observe the whole language program in action—to see the forest instead of the trees, so to speak. A few minutes of observation each day can reaffirm a teacher's faith in the students and the whole language process. Taking this time is as important as any other aspect of assessment and evaluation. There are a number of ways to organize observations, but the main point is to keep these general observations constant, no matter what form they take.

Monday 12/6
Red group.—John on task
Sue " "
Bill " "
Tuesday 12/7
Blue group— Zak task related

Island of the Blue Dolphins is like Hatchet because of the survival stuff.
I liked Hatchet better.

Tippy finished her math assignment and chose to read a book.

Observe Small Groups
Anecdotal records indicate children on/off task or task-related activities in a five-minute period.

Record Student Observations
Listen to student remarks to each other and record significant or telling statements.

Specific Behavior
Record a child's specific behavior and show how he or she makes transitions from one activity to another.

To make this assessment process manageable, individual observations can be written on white peel-off labels. These observations should be dated and placed on the students' pages in a teacher's log.

Write observations on peel-off labels.

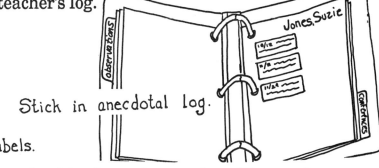

Stick in anecdotal log.

This informal observation process should take no longer than fifteen minutes at a time. Informal observations can be held at different times through-

123

out the day so that students are observed performing a variety of activities. After anecdotal records are made for a five- to fifteen-minute period every few days, important patterns in student responses to whole language will begin to emerge.

CONFERENCES

Individual student conferences can be scheduled daily during reading time. While students are involved in related reading activities, a teacher can meet with students individually to discuss aspects of the story currently being read. During this time, the teacher listens to the child read aloud to ascertain fluency, word-attack skills, use of context clues to decipher unfamiliar words, basic comprehension, and any other individual skills. This time can also be used to tape record the child's reading of a passage or retelling of a story.

Conference time should not be made intimidating for students. It is merely a time for teachers to interact one-to-one with their students in order to gain a better sense of each child's individual progress. Anecdotal records can be kept during these conferences.

Conferencing Activities	Anecdotal Records
1. Children share books they are reading on their own, how they like them, favorite parts, and other books they like.	1. Teacher notes books the children like and any other significant information.
2. Read aloud. Teacher can tape record reading.	2. Teacher notes fluency, if context clues are used to decipher unfamiliar words, work attack skills, voice inflection, etc.
3. Discuss favorite school activities, including thematic units and other projects and pastimes.	3. Teacher notes responses.

> → Total time = 10-15 minutes per conference
> → Meet with 2 to 3 children a day
> → Conference with each child every 2-3 weeks

Staying in touch with students through conferences helps teachers assess individual and collective responses to the whole language process. Should parents pop in after school for a quick assessment of their child, a teacher will have a wealth of information available.

124

Many national testing companies are field-testing the integrated performance assessment. This is the perhaps the best and most holistic way of evaluating student learning in a whole language program.

This type of assessment involves conducting a good lesson that includes reading, writing, listening, and speaking activities based on a literature book or passage from a work of literature. It is usually administered in forty to sixty minute periods over a period of about two to four days. For students, the goal of this evaluation is to motivate them to think and write about their reading assignments. For teachers, the ultimate goal of the integrated performance assessment is to test their own teaching methods.

The activities are process-oriented; there are no right or wrong answers. Scoring is based upon the students' writing and determined by a rubric of attributes found in their writing. It is is often completed on the district or regional level. For example, two different teachers might score each paper and an average or combined score will be given. If there is a large discrepancy between the two scores, a third teacher will read the student's paper and make a final decision.

This approach to assessment is very effective and involves only a day or two of a teacher's time.

Over 2-4 days, children read/listen/speak/write about a story or passage. Sessions last 45-60 min.

Teacher directs and assists with lesson as she normally would.

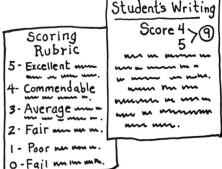

Groups of 2-6 grade teachers read and score student writing according to scoring rubric of attributes. Two teachers read each student's work.

The specific activities will vary according to the developmental level of the learners, as will the scoring process, but the basic elements of the evaluation remain much the same.

This three-part sample performance assessment is based on the book *The Napping House* by Audrey Wood. Each day's session lasts about 45 minutes.

DAY 1: Predicting, Read Book, Complete Sentence Frame

Before Reading Activities: Discuss the cover of the book, the subject of the book, and who the characters might be in the story. Write student ideas on cards and place them in a pocket chart to complete a sentence frame that reads "A _____ is sleeping." Place words on cards in the sentence frame and have the children read the sentences aloud while pointing to each word.

EXAMPLE:

A _____ is sleeping.
lady
girl   boy
dog
daddy

pocket chart with sentence frame and word cards from student discussion

Read Aloud: Read aloud *The Napping House* and direct children to listen for all the people and animals that are sleeping in the story.

After Reading Activity: Ask children who else in the story was sleeping. Write additional words on individual cards and place them one-by-one in the pocket chart story frame. Read the sentence with each new word in it, pointing to each word as the children read aloud.

Writing Assignment: Children receive a piece of paper with a duplicated sentence frame on it. They think about who they want to write about and tell the person next to them before writing. Each child completes the sentence frame and draws a picture illustrating it. The students should not receive help with spelling or punctuation.

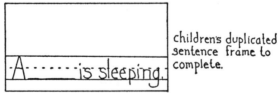

children's duplicated sentence frame to complete.

Evaluation: Children read aloud their sentences, pointing to each word if they can. Note if each child can point to each word and read it and how the filled in word is spelled. (The level of spelling indicates how much a child knows about the alphabetic principle—if it is scribbled, a string of unassociated letters, correct beginning letters, etc. All of these processes reveal the level at which the child is functioning and help the teacher adjust later instruction.)

DAY 2: Read Book, Sequence Sentence Frame

Before Reading Activity: Discuss the sequence of the story as the students remember it from the previous day. Take the previous day's word cards and manipulate them in the pocket chart on two or three sentence frames. (This will depend on the ability of the students.) The sentence frame reads: "A _____ sleeps on the _____." Read aloud with children each complete sentence while pointing to each word. Write new words on individual cards if needed. Instruct children to listen for sequence when reading story again.

EXAMPLE:

| A | girl | sleeps on the | bed | . |

A _____ sleeps on the _____ .

A _____ sleeps on the _____ .

| flea | dog | cat |

| mouse |

Read Aloud: Read aloud *The Napping House.* Children listen for the sequence of the story.

After Reading Activity: Repeat the Before Reading Activity and manipulate word cards in the pocket chart sentence frames in a sequence dictated by students. Read each sentence aloud with the children while pointing to each word.

Writing Assessment: Children receive two or three duplicated sentence frames, depending on their ability. They are to think about how they will complete and sequence them, then share with their neighbors before writing. Each child completes the sentence frames, sequences them, and draws pictures to illustrate them. The pages are then stapled into a book. The students should not be helped with spelling, punctuation, or sequencing of papers.

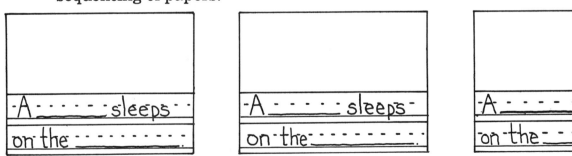

Evaluation: Children read their books to the teacher, pointing to each word if they can. Note if each child can point to each word, how the filled in words are spelled, and how events are sequenced.

DAY 3: Read Book, Write Own Sentences

Before Reading Activity: Discuss where children sleep at home and who sleeps with them (a sister, brother, cat, teddy bear, etc.). Write the sentence frame "I sleep _____." on the board. Discuss how students would complete it. Instruct them to listen to the story again and think about how they would write their own napping house story.

Read Aloud: Read aloud *The Napping House.* Remind students to think about what they will write in their own stories while listening to the story.

After Reading Activity: Discuss more ideas with which students can complete the sentence frame: "I sleep _____." Encourage creativity and the extension of ideas into more than one sentence.

Writing Assignment: Children think about the sentence or sentences they will write and share their ideas with a partner before beginning. They then copy the sentence frame from the board and complete it, adding other sentences if they wish and illustrating their work. The students are not assisted with spelling, punctuation, or completion of sentences.

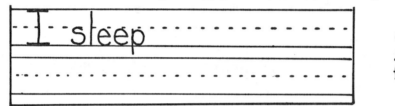

children copy sentence frame from board

Evaluation: Students read their stories to the teacher, pointing to each word if they can. Note if each child can point to each word, how sentence is completed, and how words are spelled.

The following scoring rubric can be used to assess the emergent learner's development. This type of assessment is meant to determine the level at which children are functioning to enable lessons to be better geared to their developmental levels.

SCORING RUBRIC

1 Needs Developmental Work	2 Working at Level	3 Becoming a Developing Learner
• scribbles, writes, or uses strings of letters • writes some beginning letters • has difficulty copying from board • unable to sequence events	• spaces words properly in sentence • invented spelling includes correct beginning and ending letters • writes own simple sentences • sequences two events	• invented spelling includes correct beginning, middle, and ending letters • spells some commonly used words correctly • writes two or more original sentences • sentence patterns are more complex • sequences three or more events

This three-day sample performance assessment is based on the book *William's Doll* by Charlotte Zolotow. Each day's session lasts from 45 minutes to an hour.

DAY 1: Reading—Drawing Conclusions, Predicting Outcomes, Reading Comprehension

Before Reading Activity: Discuss the title of the book and ask children what they think the story is about. Then discuss why a boy would want a doll and if having a doll would help or hurt him. Distribute duplicated pages so that students can record their own thoughts before they read the story.

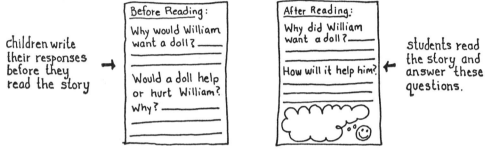

After children have recorded their ideas, direct them to the questions on the second duplicated sheet, and tell children to listen to the story with these questions in mind.

Read Story: Read aloud the story to students.

After Reading Activity: Children answer the questions on their After Reading sheet and illustrate their answers if they wish.

Writing Assignment: Ask children to think about whether or not William would be a good father and why. Discuss their reasons, then instruct them to write their ideas in the thinking cloud on the After Reading sheet.

DAY 2: Group Work—Character Analysis, Compare/Contrast, Vivid Words

Cooperative Reading Activity: In cooperative groups of four or five students each, children brainstorm ideas to answer the questions on their duplicated sheets.

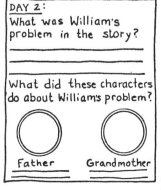
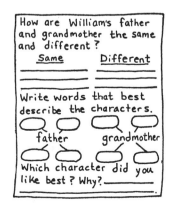

DAY 3: Writing—Character Analysis, Story Details, Summarizing

Before Reading Activity: Students individually review the cooperative group activity they completed the day before. Lead a discussion of their responses, then direct students to listen to or read the story again so they can tell it from either the father's or grandmother's point of view.

Read Story: Either read aloud *William's Doll* or let students read it for themselves.

Writing Activity: Students write the story from either the father's or grandmother's point of view on a clean sheet of paper.

Evaluation: Evaluate the three-day process by reading and scoring student work according to a developing learners' scoring rubric. Consolidate student papers by grade level and have two different teachers read and score each student's work. If the teachers' scores disagree by 2 points or more, have a third teacher read and score the paper. These assessments are meant primarily to determine the type of additional instruction students may need. Class, school, or district minimum scores may be helpful when assessing students' writing abilities.

SCORING RUBRIC

Developing Learners
5 - Sentences vary in length and complexity. Uses vivid words and conventional spelling, capitalization and punctuation. Shows exceptional understanding of story and goes beyond details to show insight into character.
4 - Sentences show a good degree of complexity. Spells most words correctly. Most capitalization and punctuation rules observed. Shows very good understanding of story and uses details when revealing character.
3 - Sentences of average length and complexity. Spells many words correctly. Basic capitalization and punctuation rules observed. Story details understood enough to reveal character.
2 - Sentences vary between simple and slightly more complex. Some words spelled correctly; otherwise uses invented spelling. Some capitalization and punctuation mistakes. Basic story details somewhat understood.
1 - Simple sentence structure. Uses only invented spelling and little capitalization and punctuation. Few story details understood.
0 - Unable to complete task.

This three-day sample performance assessment is based on excerpts from the book *A Wrinkle in Time* by Madeline L'Engle. Each day's session lasts approximately 45 minutes or an hour.

DAY 1: Reading—Summarizing, Mood, Main Idea, Analyze Character/Setting, Compare/Contrast

Before Reading Activity: Distribute to students an excerpt from the first chapter of *A Wrinkle in Time*. The passage begins with, "It was a dark and stormy night . . ." and ends with, "It's a privilege, not a punishment." Explain that a strange mood is established in the passage. Then ask students to read the passage to identify how the setting establishes the main character's mood.

Students Read: Students read the passage themselves and are encouraged to make notes about their thoughts while reading.

After Reading Activity: Students write answers to questions about the passage.

DAY 2: Group Work—Mood, Brainstorming, Summarizing, Vivid Words, Mapping Ideas

Small Group Activity: In small groups of four or five each, students complete the next set of duplicated pages.

DAY 3: Writing—Mechanics, Organizing Ideas, Vivid Words

Writing Activity: Students use the map they completed the day before and add to it if they wish to organize their thoughts before writing. Encourages them to use vivid words and correct spelling and punctuation. Students write their stories.

Evaluation: Two teachers read and score student work according to the fluent learners' scoring rubric. Separate scores for reading and writing are given. If the teachers' scores differ by two points or more, a third teacher should read and score the paper. These scores are helpful in diagnosing and addressing student weaknesses. They may also be effectively used as minimum scores for passing or retaining students in intermediate grades and middle schools.

SCORING RUBRIC

Fluent Learners — Reading	Fluent Learners — Writing
5 - *Excellent.* Exceptional understanding of passage. Gleans unusual insight from ideas conveyed and extends them beyond confines of text. May even challenge aspects of the passage.	5 - *Excellent.* Exceptional organization and command of written language. Uses vivid, compelling sentences. No errors in spelling, grammar, or punctuation.
4 - *Commendable.* Shows very good understanding of passage significance. Extends and applies knowledge, but level of intensity may vary between questions.	4 - *Commendable.* Sentences show a good degree of complexity and are correctly written. Very good organization of ideas. Few errors, if any, in spelling, grammar, or punctuation.
3 - *Average.* Understands significance of text beyond basic comprehension. Gives accurate summary of facts. Makes some extensions and applications.	3 - *Average.* Sentences of regular length and complexity. Minor organizational flaws, but ideas flow logically. Some errors in sentence, grammar, or punctuation.
2 - *Fair.* Basic literal comprehension, but little else. Can retell plot, but with some inaccuracies.	2 - *Fair.* Sentences show little variety. Some sense of organization evident, but focus is unclear. Several errors in sentence structure, spelling, grammar, and punctuation
1 - *Poor.* Little sense of basic comprehension. Factual errors apparent. Copies information from text.	1 - *Poor.* No sentence variety. No evidence of organization or focus. Many errors in sentence structure, spelling, grammar, and punctuation.
0 - *Fail.* Unable to complete task.	0 - *Fail.* Unable to complete task.

STANDARDIZED TESTING

Although the integrated performance assessment is an excellent means of accurately determining a child's whole language skills, it is important to have a wider scope of student achievement. Standardized norm-referenced tests provide national percentile rankings by student, school, and district. To keep a balance between specific individual student abilities and a wider view of how they compare to others across the nation, a limited use of standardized testing is recommended.

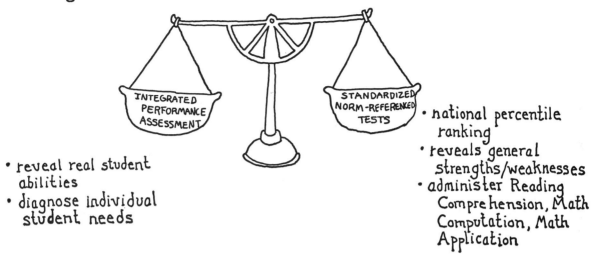

- reveal real student abilities
- diagnose individual student needs

- national percentile ranking
- reveals general strengths/weaknesses
- administer Reading Comprehension, Math Computation, Math Application

The three standardized tests which are most useful to the teacher are reading comprehension, math computation, and math applications. Teachers may want to administer these tests at every grade (K-6), or in specific grades for a general indication of program achievement (test is administered in grades 2 and 5 only, for example).

A recent addition to educational evaluation is the enhanced multiple choice test. This multiple choice test provides students with information through a number of media (for example, a passage, a map, and a chart) and then asks students to think critically about the types of questions they can answer from the information available.

From the information provided what kinds of things can you learn about Amanda's trip?

o When she left home.
o What day it is.
o What train she is taking
o Where she has to be Saturday.
o What time the Salt Lake City train leaves.

With these kinds of advancements in educational testing, a student's whole language abilities and thinking skills can now be assessed more adequately than ever.

Chapter Eleven

PARENTS AS PARTNERS

Effective communication with parents and making parents a part of the learning process are important aspects of every whole language program. Both of these areas need to be addressed in order to elicit the home support necessary for real learning to take place.

EFFECTIVE COMMUNICATION

Parents tend to judge their children's classrooms by their own elementary and middle school experiences. If they do not understand the basic tenets of a whole language program, they will not understand the processes and activities their children are undergoing. The teacher needs to discuss with parents the concept of whole language instruction, but recent developments in teaching theories and classroom practices should be explained in plain English. Education jargon such as "emergent," "developing," or "fluent" should be avoided when possible. The best way to introduce parents to the theory of whole language is to provide them with many examples of the types of student work they can expect to see coming home.

Parents can receive a good idea of how a whole language program works during a Back to School Night. By visiting the classroom, parents come to understand how all of the elements in a whole language classroom work together and can observe first-hand the classroom's environment and materials. On a regular basis, teachers should send home letters that detail classroom activities. Only through sustained communication can parents come to fully embrace the whole language program and become and integral part of their own child's learning process.

Parent involvement is essential to the success of a whole language program and can be implemented in a variety of ways. Although many parents work and are unable to devote a great deal of time to the classroom, there are numerous alternatives available which allow them to stay in touch with their children's learning. Wish lists, class newsletters, parent volunteers, book bags, and home study areas all provide a means for parents to get involved.

WISH LISTS

Wish lists are lists of materials the class needs for upcoming projects. If teachers send home wish lists they may be surprised at the response, even in the most depressed neighborhoods. Most parents want to help their child's classrooms but can't volunteer time. Sending needed supplies to school makes them feel as if they are participating in the program—and they are!

Sending wish lists home quarterly can be very helpful. Inviting parents to drop in on a display of class projects every quarter also helps promote interest in the whole language program.

A weekly, bi-weekly, or even monthly class newsletter keeps parents apprised of classroom activities. A newsletter also provides a direct format for soliciting parent help for special projects which do not require long-term commitments.

Room 5 Newsletter
Everybody Reads !!!

This is the concept we are learning about. Can you come by and share something you read in the next few weeks?

I will share ____ (type of book)
(day & time) ____ (name/phone)

INVENTED SPELLING ★ ★ ★
Invented spelling is the process children go through to learn to spell. Think of it as "under construction".
THEMES STUDIED + + + +

Fluent learner reading groups can compile the newsletter in class or on a school computer. Or a parent can type it at home as a way of volunteering time.

Students of all ages can submit poems, articles, and drawings for the newsletter in a box, and parent volunteers, older students, or reading groups (in the case of fluent learners) can compile the submissions at the end of the week. This work can be done by students on a class or school computer (there are some good software programs for newsletters), or by a parent volunteer at home. Students enjoy contributing to class newsletters, but the project must be kept comfortably manageable for the teacher if it is to be effective.

PARENT VOLUNTEERS

Parents can volunteer their time in a number of ways. One of the most effective arrangements is to have parents visit the classroom for a few hours each week. Teachers can easily work these volunteers into their whole language programs by placing them in small groups to help with individual students or to prepare materials for class projects. Unfortunately, many parents who would like to help are not available on a regular basis. For them, there are many other ways to volunteer.

Volunteer on a weekly basis.

Volunteer a lunch hour a week/bi-weekly to read aloud to kids.

Prepare class projects/newsletters at home.

Give 15-minute book talks periodically.

Participate in one class project.

Donate needed materials to school.

Drive on one or more fieldtrips.

Organize local businesses to donate time/material for projects.

Select/organize library books around a theme being studied.

Record tapes for listening center at home.

Spearhead parent drive to buy a class set of needed books.

Do the legwork for organizing a field-trip.

BOOK BAGS

If parents are unable to help with class projects either at home or at school, they will usually make time for activities which involve their own children. Book bags provide a means for children to take home a book, read it to their parents, or have their parents read it to them. A book bag can be as simple or elaborate as teachers and students want to make them—from zip-closing plastic bags to decorated canvas totes. The idea is for the child to get the book home and read or listen to it. Notes can go home along with the books so that parents and other family members can notify the teacher that they have heard their child read.

Parent reads aloud to child.

Child reads book aloud to three people.

Child reads chapter aloud to parents.

HOME STUDY AREAS

Parents should be encouraged to arrange a comfortable, accessible study area at home for their children. The attributes of a good home study area can be outlined at a Back to School Night or other parent meetings as well as in class newsletters or other flyers sent home.

A home study area should include:

1. A quiet place for the child to read, study, and do homework. It should be well-lit and removed from the television, radio, and other distractions.

2. A variety of reading material should be accessible (books, magazines, newspapers, reference material).

138

3. A variety of writing material should be made available (pens, pencils, felt pens, lined/blank paper).

4. Children should be encouraged to express their ideas verbally and in writing.

5. Children should read or be read to daily. Family members should model reading as a life skill.

Teachers may want to develop this list into a checklist to be sent home to parents.

With parents as partners in the whole language process, students have the best of all possible worlds. The skills they practice in the classroom and see modeled by parents and family members at home become part of their own lives. When this happens, we will come closer to having the thriving literate society our democracy requires.

Chapter Twelve

BOOK LISTS

EMERGENT LEARNER BOOK LIST

Emergent learners need a great deal of exposure to wordless and predictable books that enhance the connection between the written and spoken word. They also need to view their teacher model storytelling from wordless books as this action helps them to comprehend the different parts of stories and to later model the stories for themselves.

WORDLESS BOOKS

The Adventures of Paddy Pork by John Goodall

Ah-Choo! by Mercer Mayer

The Angel and the Soldier Boy by Peter Collington

Anno's Journey by Mitsumasa Anno

Bobo's Dream by Martha Alexander

A Boy, a Dog and a Frog by Mercer Mayer

Bubble, Bubble by Mercer Mayer

Changes, Changes by Pat Hutchins

The City by Douglas Florian

Creepy Castle by John Goodall

Deep in the Forest by Brinton Turkle

Do Not Disturb by Nancy Tafuri

Do You Want to Be My Friend? by Eric Carle

Dreams by Peter Spier

Ernest and Celestine's Patchwork Quilt by Gabrielle Vincent

The Gift by John Prater

Good Dog Carl by Alexandra Day

The Grey Lady and the Strawberry Snatcher by Molly Bang

Hanimals by Mario Mariotti

Hanimations by Mario Mariotti

Jungle Walk by Nancy Tafuri

Little Red Riding Hood by John Goodall

Look Again by Tana Hoban

Moonlight by Jan Ormerod

Noah's Ark by Peter Spier

The Other Bone by Ed Young

Pancakes for Breakfast by Tomie dePaola

Peter Spier's Christmas by Peter Spier

Peter Spier's Rain by Peter Spier

Picnic by Emily McCully

Rosie's Walk by Pat Hutchins

The Snowman by Raymond Briggs

The Story of a Castle by John Goodall

The Story of an English Village by John Goodall

The Story of Little Mouse Trapped in a Book by Monique Felix

Sunshine by Jan Ormerod

Truck by David Crews

26 Letters and 99 Cents by Tana Hoban

Up a Tree by Ed Young

Are You My Mother? by P.D. Eastman

Ask Mister Bear by Marjorie Flack

Bringing the Rain to Kapiti Plain by Verna Aardema

Brown Bear, Brown Bear, What Do You See? by Bill Martin, Jr.

Chicken Soup with Rice by Maurice Sendak

A Dark, Dark Tale by Ruth Brown

Do You Want to Be My Friend? by Eric Carle

The Doorbell Rang by Pat Hutchins

Fortunately by Remy Charlip

The Gingerbread Boy by Paul Galdone

Goodnight Moon by Margaret Wise Brown

Hattie and the Fox by Mem Fox

Henny Penny by Paul Galdone

The House That Jack Built by Rodney Peppe

I Was Walking Down the Road by Sarah Barchas

Jesse Bear, What Will You Wear? by Nancy Carlstrom

Jump, Frog, Jump! by Robert Kalan

King Bidgood's in the Bathtub by Audrey Wood

The Little Old Lady Who Was Not Afraid of Anything by Linda Williams

Old Mother Hubbard by Colin and Jacqui Hawkins

One Monday Morning by Uri Schulevitz

Over in the Meadow by Olive Wadsworth

The Napping House by Audrey Wood

Rain Makes Applesauce by Julian Scheer

The Rose in My Garden by Arnold Lobel

The Teeny Tiny Woman by Barbara Seuling

Three Blind Mice by John Ivimey

The Three Little Pigs by Paul Galdone

This Old Man: The Counting Song by Robin Koontz

Tikki Tikki Tembo by Arlene Mosel

The Very Busy Spider by Eric Carle

The Wheels on the Bus by Mary Ann Kovalski

Where's Spot? by Eric Hill

Who Sank the Boat? by Pamela Allen

Why Mosquitoes Buzz in People's Ears by Verna Aardema

PICTURE BOOKS

Abel's Island by William Steig

Alexander and the Terrible, Horrible, No Good, Very Bad Day by Judith Viorst

Alexander and the Wind-Up Mouse by Leo Lionni

Alexander, Who Used to Be Rich Last Sunday by Judith Viorst

The Amazing Bone by William Steig

Amelia Bedelia by Peggy Parish

Amos and Boris by William Steig

And to Think That I Saw It on Mulberry Street by Dr. Seuss

Animalia by Graeme Base

Animals Born Alive and Well by Ruth Heller

Animals Should Definitely Not Wear Clothing by Judy Barrett

Annie and the Old One by Miska Miles

Anno's Counting Book by Mitsumasa Anno

Another Mouse to Feed by Robert Kraus

The Art Lesson by Tomie dePaola

Barn Dance! by Bill Martin, Jr.

Bedtime for Frances by Russell Hoban

Ben's Dream by Chris Van Allsburg

Big Bad Bruce by Bill Peet

The Biggest Bear by Lynd Ward

The Biggest House in the World by Leo Lionni

Bill and Pete by Tomie dePaola

Bill and Pete Go Down the Nile by Tomie dePaola

Blueberries for Sal by Robert McCloskey

The Book of Pigericks by Arnold Lobel

Bored–Nothing to Do! by Peter Spier

The Boy Who Held Back the Sea by Thomas Locker

Bread and Jam for Frances by Russell Hoban

Bringing the Rain to Kapiti Plain by Verna Aardema

Brown Bear, Brown Bear, What Do You See? by Bill Martin, Jr.

The Butter Battle Book by Dr. Seuss

Caps for Sale by Esphyr Slobodkina

Carousel by Donald Crews

The Carrot Seed by Ruth Krauss

Castle by David Macaulay

The Cat in the Hat by Dr. Seuss

Cathedral by David Macaulay

City by David Macaulay

A Chair for My Mother by Vera Williams

Cherries and Cherry Pits by Vera Williams

Chester, the Worldly Pig by Bill Peet

Chick Chick a Boom Boom by Bill Martin, Jr.

Chicken Soup with Rice by Maurice Sendak

Chickens Aren't the Only Ones by Ruth Heller

A Chocolate Moose for Dinner by Fred Gwynne

Clancy's Coat by Eve Bunting

Clementina's Cactus by Ezra Jack Keats

Cloudy with a Chance of Meatballs by Judy Barrett

A Color of His Own by Leo Lionni

Corduroy by Don Freeman

Crictor by Tomi Ungerer

Crow Boy by Taro Yashima

Curious George by H.A. Rey

Dandelion by Don Freeman

Danny and the Dinosaur by Syd Hoff

The Day Jimmy's Boa Ate the Wash by Trinka Noble

Dinosaur Bob and His Adventures with the Family Lizard by William Joyce

Dinosaur Time by Peggy Parish

Dinosaurs by Gail Gibbons

Doctor DeSoto by William Steig

Draw Me a Star by Eric Carle

The Eleventh Hour: A Curious Mystery by Graeme Base

The Erie Canal by Peter Spier

Fables by Arnold Lobel

Fish Is Fish by Leo Lionni

Flash, Crash, Rumble and Roll by Franklyn Branley

Foolish Rabbit's Big Mistake by Rafe Martin

Fox in Socks by Dr. Seuss

The Fox Went Out on a Chilly Night by Peter Spier

Frederick by Leo Lionni

Freight Train by Donald Crews

Funnybones by Janet and Allan Ahlberg

George and Martha by James Marshall

The Giving Tree by Shel Silverstein

Goodnight Moon by Margaret Wise Brown

Gorilla by Anthony Browne

Green Eggs and Ham by Dr. Seuss

The Grouchy Ladybug by Eric Carle

Have You Seen My Cat? by Eric Carle

Harry and the Terrible Whatzit by Dick Gackenbach

Harry the Dirty Dog by Gene Zion

Hawk, I'm Your Brother by Byrd Baylor

Heckedy Peg by Audrey Wood

Hector Protector, and as I Went Over the Water by Maurice Sendak

Hop on Pop by Dr. Seuss

Horton Hears a Who by Dr. Seuss

A House for Hermit Crab by Eric Carle

A House Is a House for Me by Mary Ann Hoberman

How a Book Is Made by Aliki

How I Hunted the Little Fellows by Boris Zhitkov

How the Grinch Stole Christmas! by Dr. Seuss

I Like Books by Anthony Browne

If I Ran the Zoo by Dr. Seuss

If You Give a Mouse a Cookie by Laura Numeroff

I'll Fix Anthony by Judith Viorst

Inch by Inch by Leo Lionni

Ira Sleeps Over by Bernard Waber

Island Boy by Barbara Cooney

The Island of the Skog by Steven Kellogg

Jimmy's Boa Bounces Back by Trinka Hakes Noble

Johnny Appleseed: A Tall Tale by Steven Kellogg

The Jolly Postman by Janet and Allan Ahlberg

Jumanji by Chris Van Allsburg

Katy and the Big Snow by Virginia Lee Burton

Kermit the Hermit by Bill Peet

The Kids' Cat Book by Tomie dePaola

King Bidgood's in the Bathtub by Audrey Wood

The King Who Rained by Fred Gwynne

Knots on a Counting Rope by Bill Martin, Jr.

Koko's Kitten by Dr. Francine Patterson

Left Handed Shortstop by Patricia Reilly Giff

The Legend of the Bluebonnet by Tomie dePaola

Let's Make Rabbits by Leo Lionni

A Letter to Amy by Ezra Jack Keats

Little Bear by Else Holmelund Minarik

Little Blue and Little Yellow by Leo Lionni

The Little Engine That Could by Watty Piper

The Little House by Virginia Lee Burton

The Little Island by Margaret W. Brown

A Little Pigeon Toad by Fred Gwynne

Little Rabbit's Loose Tooth by Lucy Bate

The Little Red Hen by Paul Galdone

Little Red Riding Hood by Trina Schart Hyman

The Lorax by Dr. Seuss

Madeline by Ludwig Bemelmans

Maggie and the Pirate by Ezra Jack Keats

The Magic School Bus at the Waterworks by Joanna Cole

The Magic School Bus Inside the Earth by Joanna Cole

The Magic School Bus Inside the Human Body by Joanna Cole

The Magic School Bus Lost in the Solar System by Joanna Cole

Make Way for Ducklings by Robert McCloskey

Many Luscious Lollipops by Ruth Heller

The Mare on the Hill by Thomas Locker

Meanwhile Back at the Ranch by Trinka Hakes Noble

Mike Mulligan and His Steam Shovel by Virginia Lee Burton

Mill by David Macauley

Millions of Cats by Wanda Gag

Milton the Early Riser by Robert Kraus

Ming Lo Moves the Mountain by Arnold Lobel

Miss Nelson Has a Field Day by Harry Allard

Miss Nelson Is Back by Harry Allard

Miss Nelson Is Missing by Harry Allard

Miss Rumphius by Barbara Cooney

Mr. Rabbit and the Lovely Present by Charlotte Zolotow

The Moon's Revenge by Joan Aiken

Mop Top by Don Freeman

Moss Gown by William H. Hooks

Mother Goose, A Treasury of Best Loved Rhymes by Watty Piper

The Mother's Day Mice by Eve Bunting

The Mountain That Loved a Bird by Alice McLerran

Much Bigger Than Martin by Steven Kellogg

Mufaro's Beautiful Daughters: An African Tale by John Steptoe

My Grandson Lew by Charlotte Zolotow

My Mama Says There Aren't Any Zombies, Ghost, Vampires, Creatures, Demons, Monsters, Fiends, Goblins, or Things by Judith Viorst

The Mysteries of Harris Burdick by Chris Van Allsburg

The Mysterious Tadpole by Steven Kellogg

Nadia the Willful by Sue Alexander

Nana Upstairs and Nana Downstairs by Tomie dePaola

The Napping House by Audrey Wood

Next Year I'll Be Special by Patricia Reilly Giff

Nice Little Girls by Elizabeth Levy

Night in the Country by Cynthia Rylant

No Jumping on the Bed by Tedd Arnold

No Such Things by Bill Peet

Noah's Ark by Peter Spier

Nobody Listens to Andrew by Elizabeth Guilfoile

Now One Foot, Now the Other by Tomie dePaola

Oh, the Places You'll Go by Dr. Seuss

Oh! Were They Ever Happy! by Peter Spier

Old Mother Witch by Carol and Donald Carrick

On Beyond Zebra by Dr. Seuss

On Market Street by Arnold Lobel

On My Beach There Are Many Pebbles by Leo Lionni

Once a Mouse by Marcia Brown

One Fish, Two Fish, Red Fish, Blue Fish by Dr. Seuss

One Morning in Maine by Robert McCloskey

Owl At Home by Arnold Lobel

Owl Moon by Jane Yolen

Pamela Camel by Bill Peet

Pancakes for Breakfast by Tomie dePaola

Papa, Please Get the Moon for Me by Eric Carle

The Paper Crane by Molly Bang

Parade by Donald Crews

Patrick's Dinosaurs by Carol Carrick

People by Peter Spier

Petunia the Silly Goose Stories by Roger Duviosin

Pierre by Maurice Sendak

Piggybook by Anthony Browne

Pinkerton, Behave! by Steven Kellogg

The Pinkish, Purplish, Bluish Egg by Bill Peet

The Piped Piper of Hamelin by Barbara Bartos Hoppner

Plants That Never Bloom by Ruth Heller

The Poky Little Puppy by Janette S. Lowery

The Polar Express by Chris Van Allsburg

The Popcorn Book by Tomie dePaola

Possum Magic by Mem Fox

Princess Ugly by Jane Yolen

Pyramid by David Macaulay

The Quarreling Book by Charlotte Zolotow

The Quicksand Book by Tomie dePaola

Rain by Robert Kalan

The Reason for a Flower by Ruth Heller

Regards to the Man in the Moon by Ezra Jack Keats

Rich Cat, Poor Cat by Bernard Waber

Rip Van Winkle by retold by John Howe

Ronald Morgan Goes to Bat by Patricia Reilly Giff

Rose and Michael by Judith Viorst

A Rose for Pinkerton by Steven Kellogg

The Rose in My Garden by Arnold Lobel

Rosie's Walk by Pat Hutchins

Round Trip by Ann Jonas

Runaway Bunny by Margaret Brown

Sailing With the Wind by Thomas Locker

Say It! by Charlotte Zolotow

School Bus by Donald Crews

Secret Birthday Message by Eric Carle

Seven Little Monsters by Maurice Sendak

The Sign on Rosie's Door by Maurice Sendak

The Silver Pony by Lynd Ward

The Sixteen Hand Horse by Fred Gwynne

Sleep Out by Carol Carrick

Sky Dogs by Jan Yolen

Small Pig by Arnold Lobel

A Snake's Body by Joanna Cole

The Snowy Day by Ezra Jack Keats

Solomon the Rusty Nail by William Steig

A Special Trick by Mercer Mayer

Stevie by John Steptoe

Stone Soup by Marcia Brown

The Story of Ferdinand by Munro Leaf

The Stranger by Chris Van Allsburg

Strega Nona by Tomie dePaola

Stringbean's Trip to the Shining Sea by Vera Williams

The Stupids Step Out by Harry Allard

Swimmy by Leo Lionni

Sylvester the Magic Pebble by William Steig

The Tale of Peter Rabbit by Beatrix Potter

The Tenth Good Thing About Barney by Judith Viorst

That Terrible Halloween Night by James Stevenson

There's Nothing to Do! by James Stevenson

Thomas' Snowsuit by Robert Munsch

The Three Bears by Paul Galdone

The Three Little Pigs by Paul Galdone

Thidwick, the Big-Hearted Moose by Dr. Seuss

Thy Friend, Obadiah by Brinton Turkle

Tikki Tikki Tembo by Arlene Mosel

149

Time of Wonder by Robert McCloskey

Tintin in Tibet by Hergé

Too Many Books by Caroline Feller Bauer

A Tree Is Nice by Janice Udry

A Treeful of Pigs by Arnold Lobel

The Trek by Ann Jonas

Truck by Donald Crews

Two Bad Ants by Chris Van Allsburg

Umbrella by Taro Yashima

Unbuilding by David Macaulay

Underground by David Macaulay

The Very Busy Spider by Eric Carle

The Very Hungry Caterpillar by Eric Carle

The Very Worst Monster by Pat Hutchins

Watch Out for the Chicken Feet in Your Soup by Tomie dePaola

We the People by Peter Spier

What Happened to Patrick's Dinosaurs? by Carol Carrick

What's the Matter With Carruthers? by James Marshall

What's Under My Bed? by James Stevenson

When I Was Young in the Mountains by Cynthia Rylant

Where the River Begins by Thomas Locker

Where the Wild Things Are by Maurice Sendak

Where's Spot? by Eric Hill

The Whingdingdilly by Bill Peet

Whistle for Willie by Ezra Jack Keats

Whose Mouse Are You? by Robert Kraus

William's Doll by Charlotte Zolotow

Wolf! Wolf! by Elizabeth and Gerald Rose

Worse Than Willy! by James Stevenson

The Worst Person in the World by James Stevenson

The Wreck of the Zephyr by Chris Van Allsburg

The Wump World by Bill Peet

Yummers! by James Marshall

The Z Was Zapped by Chris Van Allsburg

The Zabajaba Jungle by William Steig

Zella, Zack and Zodiac by Bill Peet

TRANSITIONAL CHAPTER BOOKS

These books are intended for developing learners who are ready to graduate from reading picture books to short chapter books. They can also be read aloud to emergent learners who are ready to listen to longer works.

The Adventures of Ali Baba Bernstein by Johanna Hurwitz

Be a Perfect Person in Just Three Days! by Stephen Manes

The Bears on Hemlock Mountain by Alice Dalgliesh

The Beast in Ms. Rooney's Room by Patricia Reilly Giff

Bella Arabella by Liza Fosburgh

The Best Christmas Pageant Ever by Barbara Robinson

Call It Courage by Armstrong Sperry

A Certain Small Shepherd by Rebecca Caudill

Chocolate Fever by Robert K. Smith

The Courage of Sarah Noble by Alice Dalgliesh

Dexter by Clyde Robert Bulla

Did You Carry the Flag Today, Charley? by Rebecca Caudill

The Enormous Crocodile by Roald Dahl

Fantastic Mr. Fox by Roald Dahl

Freckle Juice by Judy Blume

*Frog and Toad Are Friends** by Arnold Lobel

Ginger Pye by Eleanor Estes

Help! I'm a Prisoner in the Library by Eth Clifford

The Hundred Dresses by Eleanor Estes

I'll Meet You in the Cucumbers by Lilian Moore

In the Dinosaur's Paw by Patricia Reilly Giff

The Iron Giant: A Story in Five Nights by Ted Hughes

Lafcadio, the Lion Who Shot Back by Shel Silverstein

A Lion to Guard Us by Clyde Robert Bulla

*The Littles** by John Peterson

The Lucky Stone by Lucille Clifton
The Marzipan Pig by Russell Hoban
Maurice's Room by Paula Fox
Mr. Popper's Penguins by Richard and Florence Atwater
The Mouse and the Motorcycle by Beverly Cleary
My Father's Dragon by Ruth S. Gannett
Owls in the Family by Farley Mowat
Pippi Longstocking by Astrid Lindgren
Ralph S. Mouse by Beverly Cleary
Ramona the Pest by Beverly Cleary
The Reluctant Dragon by Kenneth Grahame
Runaway Ralph by Beverly Cleary
Sara Crewe by Frances Hodgson Burnett
Sarah, Plain and Tall by Patricia MacLachlan
Seven Kisses in a Row by Patricia MacLachlan
Stone Fox by John R. Gardiner
The Stories Julian Tells by Ann Cameron
The Story of Holly and Ivy by Rumer Godden
The Twits by Roald Dahl
Wagon Wheels by Barbara Brenner
Wolf Story by William McCleery
Woof! by Allan Ahlberg

* There are a number of books in this series.

FLUENT LEARNER BOOK LIST

NOVELS

Fluent learners need experience reading silently in a number of different genres. They should also hear some of these books read aloud.

CONTEMPORARY FICTION

Arthur for the Very First Time by Patricia MacLachlan
The Best Christmas Pageant Ever by Barbara Robinson

The Black Pearl by Scott O'Dell
The Black Stallion by Walter Farley
Blue Willow by Doris Gates
The Bobbsey Twins Books by Laura Lee Hope
Bridge to Terabithia by Katherine Paterson
Charlotte's Web by E.B.White
Danny, the Champion of the World by Roald Dahl
Dear Mr. Henshaw by Beverly Cleary
Dicey's Song by Cynthia T. Voigt
Doodle and the Go Cart by Robert Burch
Encyclopedia Brown Sets the Pace by Donald Sobel
From the Mixed Up Files of Mrs. Basil E. Frankweiler by E.L. Konigsburg
The Great Brain by John D. Fitzgerald
The Hardy Boy Books by Franklin Dixon
Hatchet by Gary Paulsen
Henry and Beezus by Beverly Cleary
Henry Huggins by Beverly Cleary
The Incredible Journey by Sheila Burnford
Jacob Have I Loved by Katherine Paterson
J.T. by Jane Wagner
Julie of the Wolves by Jean George
The Little Prince by Antoine De Saint-Exupery
Midnight Fox by Betsy Byars
My Side of the Mountain by Jean George
Nancy Drew Mysteries by Carolyn Keene
And Nobody Knew They Were There by Otto Salassi
Old Yeller by Fred Gipson
One-Eyed Cat by Paula Fox
The Outsiders by S. E. Hinton
The Pinballs by Betsy Byars
Queenie Peavy by Robert Burch
Ramona and Her Father by Beverly Cleary
Ramona the Pest by Beverly Cleary
Sidewalk Stories from Wayside School by Louis Sachar
Sounder by William Armstrong
Stone Fox by John R. Gardiner
Summer of My German Soldier by Bette Green

Superfudge by Judy Blume

Tales of a Fourth Grade Nothing by Judy Blume

A Taste of Blackberries by Doris B. Smith

Walkabout by James V. Marshall

Where the Lilies Bloom by Vera and Bill Cleaver

Where the Red Fern Grows by Wilson Rawls

Zeely by Virginia Hamilton

HISTORICAL FICTION

Adam of the Road by Elizabeth J. Gray

By the Great Horn Spoon by Sid Fleischman

Call It Courage by Armstrong Sperry

The Cay by Theodore Taylor

Child of the Silent Night: The Story of Laura Bridgeman
    by Edith Fisher Hunter

The Courage of Sarah Nobel by Alice Dalgliesh

A Day No Pigs Would Die by Robert Newton Peck

I'm Deborah Sampson: A Soldier in the War of the Revolution
    by Patricia Clapp

Dragonwings by Laurence Yep

The Drinking Gourd by F. N. Monjo

I Heard the Owl Call My Name by Margaret Craven

In the Year of the Boar and Jackie Robinson by Bette Bao Lord

Introducing Shirley Braverman by Hilma Wolitzer

Island of the Blue Dolphins by Scott O'Dell

Little House in the Big Woods by Laura Ingalls Wilder

Little House on the Prairie by Laura Ingalls Wilder

My Brother Sam Is Dead by Collier, J. and C. Collier

North to Freedom by Anne Holm

Paddle-to-the-Sea by Holling C. Holling

Peppermints in the Parlor by Barbara Brooks Wallace

A Pocket Full of Seeds by Marilyn Sachs

Robin Hood, Prince of Outlaws by Bernard Miles

Roll of Thunder, Hear My Cry by Mildred Taylor

Sarah Bishod by Scott O'Dell

Sarah, Plain and Tall by Patricia MacLachlan

Sign of the Beaver by Elizabeth George Speare
Sing Down the Moon by Scott O'Dell
Summer of My German Soldier by Bette Green
The Witch of Blackbird Pond by Elizabeth George Speare
The Yearling by Marjorie K. Rawlings
Zia by Scott O'Dell

FANTASY AND SCIENCE FICTION

The BFG by Roald Dahl
Bunnicula by Deborah and James Howe
Caddie Woodlawn by Carol R. Brink
The Celery Stalks at Midnight by James Howe
The Changeling by Zilpha K. Snyder
Charlie and the Chocolate Factory by Roald Dahl
The Chocolate Touch by Patrick Skene Catling
The Cricket in Times Square by George Selden
Dandelion Wine by Ray Bradbury
Dragon Kite by Nancy Luenn
The Enormous Egg by Oliver Butterworth
Freaky Friday by Mary Rodgers
Mrs. Frisby and the Rats of Nimh by Robert C. O'Brien
The Indian in the Cupboard by Lynne Reid Banks
James and the Giant Peach by Roald Dahl
The Lion, The Witch, and the Wardrobe by C.S. Lewis
Mathilda by Roald Dahl
The Mouse and the Motorcycle by Beverly Cleary
Pearl's Promise by Frank Asch
The Phantom Tollbooth by Norton Juster
Pippi Longstocking by Astrid Lindgren
The Railway Children by Edith Nesbit
The Search for Delicious by Natalie Babbitt
The Secret Garden by Frances Hodgson Burnett
Sir Gawain and the Green Knight by Selina Hastings
A Swiftly Tilting Planet by Madeline L'Engle
Tuck Everlasting by Natalie Babbitt
Twenty and Ten by Claire H. Bishop

The Velveteen Rabbit by Margery Williams
The Whipping Boy by Sid Fleischman
The Wind in the Willows by Kenneth Grahame
Winnie the Pooh by A. A. Milne
A Wrinkle in Time by Madeline L'Engle

CLASSICS

Around the World in Eighty Days by Jules Verne
The Big Wave by Pearl S. Buck
Call of the Wild by Jack London
Count of Monte Cristo by Alexander Dumas
Diary of A Young Girl by Anne Frank
The Hobbit by J.R.R. Tolkien
Kidnapped by Robert Louis Stevenson
Lassie, Come Home by Eric Knight
Little Women by Louisa Mae Alcott
The Pearl by John Steinbeck
Profiles in Courage by John F. Kennedy
The Red Pony by John Steinbeck
Robinson Crusoe by Daniel Defoe
Story of My Life by Helen Keller

POETRY

The Best Loved Poems of the American People by Hazel Felleman
Hailstones and Halibut Bones by Mary O'Neill
If I Were in Charge of the World by Judith Viorst
The New Kid on the Block, Jack Prelutsky, ed.
Now We Are Six by A. A. Milne
The Random House Book of Poetry for Children, Jack Prelutsky, ed.
See My Lovely Poison Ivy by Lilian Moore
Where the Sidewalk Ends by Shel Silverstein

BIBLIOGRAPHY

Anderson, Richard C., et al. *Becoming a Nation of Readers: The Report of the Commission on Reading.* Champaign, IL: University of Illinois, Center for the Study of Reading, 1985.

Batzle, Janine. *Portfolio Assessment and Evaluation.* Cypress, CA: Creative Teaching Press, 1992.

Bauer, Karen and Rosa Drew. *Alternatives to Worksheets.* Cypress, CA: Creative Teaching Press, 1992.

Butler, Andrea. *Guided Reading.* Crystal Lake, IL: Rigby Education, 1988.

——. *Shared Book Experience: An Introduction.* Crystal Lake, IL: Rigby Education, 1987.

Cochran, Judith. *Insights to Literature, Middle Grades.* Nashville, TN: Incentive Publications, 1990.

——. *Insights to Literature, Primary.* Nashville, TN: Incentive Publications, 1991.

——. *Incorporating Literature into the Basal Reading Program.* Nashville, TN: Incentive Publications, 1991.

——. *Integrating Science and Literature.* Nashville, TN: Incentive Publications, 1992.

——. *Using Literature to Learn about Children Around the World.* Nashville, TN: Incentive Publications, 1993.

——. *Using Literature to Learn about the First Americans.* Nashville, TN: Incentive Publications, 1993.

——. *What to Do with the Gifted Child.* Nashville, TN: Incentive Publications, 1992.

Comfort, Claudette Hegel. *The Newbery-Caldecott Books in the Classroom.* Nashville, TN: Incentive Publications, 1991.

Cook, Shirley. *Linking Literature and Comprehension: Integrating Literature into Basic Skills Programs.* Nashville, TN: Incentive Publications, Inc., 1992.

———. *Linking Literature with Self-Esteem: Integrating Literature into Basic Skills Programs.* Nashville, TN: Incentive Publications, Inc., 1992.

Cook, Shirley and Kathy Carl. *Linking Literature and Writing: Integrating Literature into Basic Skills Programs.* Nashville, TN: Incentive Publications, Inc., 1989.

Elkind, David. *The Hurried Child: Growing Up Too Soon Too Fast.* Reading, MA: Addison-Wesley, 1981.

Elementary Grades Task Force Report. *It's Elementary!* Sacramento, CA: California Department of Education, 1992.

Eisele, Beverly. *Managing the Whole Language Classroom.* Cypress, CA: Creative Teaching Press, 1991.

Farr, Beverly and Roger. *Integrated Assessment System: Language Arts Performance Assessment.* New York, NY: The Psychological Corporation, HBJ, 1990.

Fader, Daniel. *The New Hooked on Books.* New York, NY: Berkeley Publishing Corporation, 1982.

Fehring, Heather and Valerie Thomas. *The Teaching of Spelling.* Crystal Lake, IL: Rigby Education, 1987.

Forte, Imogene. *From A to Z with Books and Me.* Nashville, TN: Incentive Publications, Inc., 1991.

Forte, Imogene and Joy MacKenzie. *Celebrate with Books: Literature-based Whole Language Units for Seasons and Holidays.* Nashville, TN: Incentive Publications, Inc., 1991.

Gentry, J. Richard. *Spel . . . Is a Four-Letter Word.* Portsmouth, NH: Heinemann Educational Books, Inc., 1987.

Goodman, Ken. *What's Whole in Whole Language?* Portsmouth, NH: Heinemann Educational Books, Inc., 1986.

Goodman, Ken, Yetta Goodman, and Wendy Hood, eds. *The Whole Language Evaluation Book.* Portsmouth, NH: Heinemann Educational Books, Inc., 1989.

Hornsby, David, Deborah Sukarna and Jo-Ann Parry. *Read On: A Conference Approach to Reading.* Portsmouth, NH: Heinemann Educational Books, Inc., 1988.

Hirsch, E.D., Jr. *Cultural Literacy: What Every American Needs to Know.* Boston: Houghton Mifflin, 1987.

Hunter, Madeline, Dr. *Increasing Learning Through Effective Practice.* Sacramento, CA: California Elementary Education Association, 1987.

Integrated Assessment System: Understanding Performance Assessment. New York, NY: The Psychological Corporation, 1991.

Jasmine, Julia. *Portfolio Assessment for Your Whole Language Classroom.* Huntington Beach, CA: Teacher Created Materials, Inc., 1992.

McCracken, Robert A. and Marlene J. *Reading Is Only the Tiger's Tail.* Kimberly, British Columbia, Canada: Classroom Publications, 1985.

McCracken, Robert A. and Marlene J. *Spelling Through Phonics.* Winnipeg, Manitoba, Canada: Peguis Publishers, Ltd., 1990.

Modesto City Schools. *Language Arts Performance Assessment, Grades 1-4.* Modesto, CA: Modesto City Schools, 1991.

Manning, Gary and Maryann, eds. *Whole Language: Beliefs and Practices, K-8.* Washington D.C.: National Education Association, 1989.

National Commission on Excellence in Education. *A Nation at Risk: The Imperative for Educational Reform.* Washington, D.C. U.S. Department of Education, 1983.

Newkirk, Thomas and Nancie Atwell, eds. *Understanding Writing: Ways of Observing, Learning, and Teaching.* Portsmouth, NH: Heinemann Educational Books, Inc., 1988.

Parry, Jo-Ann and David Hornsby. *Write On: A Conference Approach to Writing.* Portsmouth, NH: Heinemann Educational Books, Inc., 1989.

Pelphrey, Jo Ann. *Into the Think Tank with Literature.* Nashville, TN: Incentive Publications, Inc., 1992.

Preview CTBS: Comprehensive Tests of Basic Skills, Complete Battery. Fourth Edition. New York, NY: CTB McGraw-Hill, 1989.

Sonoma Valley Unified School District. *If You're Gonna Teach Literature, You Gotta Have This Book.* Sonoma, CA: Sonoma Valley Unified School District, 1989.

Stewig, John. *Read to Write.* New York, NY: Richard C. Owen Publishers, Inc., 1980.

Research about Teaching and Learning. Compiled by the U.S. Department of Education. Washington, D.C.: Department of Education, 1986.

Recommended Readings in Literature. Sacramento, CA: California State Department of Education, 1986.

Student Essays Illustrating the CAP Rhetorical Effectiveness Scoring System. Sacramento, CA: California State Department of Education, 1989.

Trelease, Jim. *The New Read-Aloud Handbook.* New York, NY: Penguin, 1989.

Wells, Gordon. *The Meaning Makers: Children Learning Language and Using Language to Learn.* Portsmouth, NH: Heinemann Educational Books, Inc., 1986.